# International Development and Public Religion

# American Society of Missiology Monograph Series

Series Editor, James R. Krabill

The ASM Monograph Series provides a forum for publishing quality dissertations and studies in the field of missiology. Collaborating with Pickwick Publications—a division of Wipf and Stock Publishers of Eugene, Oregon—the American Society of Missiology selects high quality dissertations and other monographic studies that offer research materials in mission studies for scholars, mission and church leaders, and the academic community at large. The ASM seeks scholarly work for publication in the series that throws light on issues confronting Christian world mission in its cultural, social, historical, biblical, and theological dimensions.

Missiology is an academic field that brings together scholars whose professional training ranges from doctoral-level preparation in areas such as Scripture, history and sociology of religions, anthropology, theology, international relations, interreligious interchange, mission history, inculturation, and church law. The American Society of Missiology, which sponsors this series, is an ecumenical body drawing members from Independent and Ecumenical Protestant, Catholic, Orthodox, and other traditions. Members of the ASM are united by their commitment to reflect on and do scholarly work relating to both mission history and the present-day mission of the church. The ASM Monograph Series aims to publish works of exceptional merit on specialized topics, with particular attention given to work by younger scholars, the dissemination and publication of which is difficult under the economic pressures of standard publishing models.

Persons seeking information about the ASM or the guidelines for having their dissertations considered for publication in the ASM Monograph Series should consult the Society's website—www.asmweb.org.

Members of the ASM Monograph Committe who approved this book are:

Paul V. Kollman, University of Notre Dame
Gary Simpson, Luther Seminary, St. Paul, MN
Michael A. Rynkiewich, Retired from Asbury Theological Seminary

RECENTLY PUBLISHED IN THE ASM MONOGRAPH SERIES

Byungohk Lee, *Listening to the Neighbor: From A Missional Perspective of the Other*

Keon-Sang An, *An Ethiopian Reading of the Bible: Biblical Interpretation of the Ethipoian Orthodox Tewahido Church*

Birgit Herppich, *Pitfalls of Trained Incapicity: The Unintended Effects of Missionary Training in the Basel Mission on Its Early Work in Ghana (1828–1840)*

# International Development and Public Religion
*Changing Dynamics of Christian Mission in South Korea*

HAEMIN LEE

☙PICKWICK *Publications* · Eugene, Oregon

INTERNATIONAL DEVELOPMENT AND PUBLIC RELIGION
Changing Dynamics of Christian Mission in South Korea

American Society of Missiology Monograph Series 27

Copyright © 2016 Haemin Lee. All rights reserved. Except for brief quotations in critical publications or reviews, no part of this book may be reproduced in any manner without prior written permission from the publisher. Write: Permissions, Wipf and Stock Publishers, 199 W. 8th Ave., Suite 3, Eugene, OR 97401.

Pickwick Publications
An Imprint of Wipf and Stock Publishers
199 W. 8th Ave., Suite 3
Eugene, OR 97401

www.wipfandstock.com

PAPERBACK ISBN 13: 978-1-4982-3989-9
HARDCOVER ISBN 13: 978-1-4982-3991-2

*Cataloguing-in-Publication data:*

Lee, Haemin

International development and public religion : changing dynamics of Christian mission in South Korea / Haemin Lee.

viii + 132 pp. ; 23 cm. Includes bibliographical references.

ISBN: 978-1-4982-3989-9 (paperback) | ISBN: 978-1-4982-3991-2 (hardback)

American Society of Missiology Monograph Series 27

1. Christianity—Korea (South). 2. Missions—Korea (South). I. Title. II. Series.

BV3460 L425 2016

Manufactured in the U.S.A.  02/18/2016

# Contents

*Preface* | vii

    Introduction | 1
1. A Brief Historical Summary of Korean Christianity | 16
2. Introducing Three Korean Organizations: Global Mission Society (GMS), Korea Food for the Hungry International (KFHI) and Good Neighbors (GN) | 32
3. History of Mission with a Special Focus on the History of the Humanitarian Dimension of Christian Mission with Respect to South Korea | 39
4. Theology of Mission and Practical Theology | 51
5. The Rise of Korean Christian Humanitarian NGOs and its Implications in Sociology of Religion and International Development | 82
6. From "Development or Mission" to "Development as Mission"? | 115

*Bibliography* | 125

# Preface

SINCE THE MID- TO late twentieth century, Christianity in the Third World has grown exponentially in size and influence, becoming increasingly polycentric—with many centers around the globe. In this process, the rise of faith-based, humanitarian, international, non-governmental organizations (NGOs) has become one of the most phenomenal trends. While traveling to more than 70 different countries in Africa, Asia, and Latin America, I have eye-witnessed the emerging surge of faith-based NGOs all around the world. This prompted me to study the relationship between religion and international development. In this book, I explore the role that religion plays in encountering secular society from various angles by drawing upon discourses in mission studies, sociology of religion, and anthropology of development. Specifically, I probe into the development practices of two major Korean organizations, Korea Food for the Hungry International (KFHI) and Good Neighbors (GN). This book investigates the following hypothesis: in terms of its emerging form, humanitarian care through international development NGOs appears to be the growing interest of Korean Christian mission and this shows a new direction of Korean Christianity as public religion. However, on closer examination, a more complex reality emerges in which diverse theological and developmental ideals motivate the Korean NGOs' humanitarian efforts. This research suggests that Korean Christians' involvement in humanitarian mission has become prominent since the early 1990s spurred by changing socio-cultural, political, and economic climates in and out of Korea. As a result, the goal of Christian mission has shifted from being unidirectional to multidirectional, which now includes humanitarian enterprises that challenge global problems including poverty, disease, and illiteracy. It reveals the diversifying theological and developmental trends of Korean Christian humanitarian mission. In terms of its mission theology, KFHI represents the holistic evangelical theology that underscores both proclamation of the gospel and serving those in need. This differs from GN's humanitarian approach that highlights the universal love of God, which inspires Christians to serve others without ulterior motives. With regard to the diversifying trends in developmental approach, KFHI undertakes its development operations by mobilizing Korean Christian churches around the world, thus being strongly ecclesial, whereas GN takes an inclusive approach that embraces development partners regardless of faith tradition. KFHI and GN therefore illustrate some of the reasons why it is important to consider international development as a crucial part of Korean Christian mission. I am grateful to all Christian mission workers who provided me with countless stories, insights, and inspirations along this enriching journey.

# Introduction

## MOTIVATIONS BEHIND THIS PROJECT

THERE ARE SEVERAL THEORETICAL and practical reasons why I decided to explore the dynamics of Korean Christians' global humanitarian mission. The first theoretical influence on me is derived from Philip Jenkins's work on global Christianity. Jenkins's book, *The Next Christendom: the Coming of Global Christianity,* has become essential reading for many students and scholars of sociology of religion and mission studies. The shift of centers of gravity is one of the major concepts that Jenkins has sensationalized. Its premise is that over the past century the center of gravity of Christianity has turned southward, to Africa, Asia, and Latin America.[1] In other words, Christianity is rapidly growing in numbers in the global South whereas it is barely surviving in the global North. Thus, Jenkins believes that the center of gravity of the Christian world has already shifted to the Southern Hemisphere. Furthermore, Jenkins shows that the churches that have grown most rapidly in Africa, Asia, and Latin America tend to be more "conservative, supernatural, and apocalyptic" compared to their northern counterparts, which have become "secular, rational, and tolerant."[2] In this, Jenkins predicts that unless the countries in the global South undergo similar types of secularization and modernization that Western countries have encountered—thus becoming more liberal and formal—the current religious trend could potentially lead to a catastrophic warfare between Christianity and Islam.[3] Jenkins also provides historical reasons why Christianity in Korea has become suc-

---

1. Jenkins, *Next Christendom,* 2.
2. Ibid., 8, 78, 107, and 162.
3. Ibid., 13.

cessful. In doing this, he mostly relies upon the historical development of Korean Christianity and argues that the remarkable success story of Korean Christianity resulted largely from its "willingness to stand up and suffer for democratic rights and for nationalist causes."[4] However, even a cursory look at his analysis raises a fundamental question: what about economic, geopolitical, socio-cultural, and religious factors behind the growth of Christianity in Korea? For example, it is very likely that Korea's political economy, which has been greatly influenced by American investors and politicians, has something to do with the rapid growth of Christianity. In addition, religious factors such as Koreans' hunger for spiritual renewal may need to be taken into account. In this, Jenkins' claim, despite its certain historical plausibility, cannot avoid the criticism of being simplistic. Moreover, the increasing number, influence, and popularity of Korean Christian humanitarian non-governmental organizations (NGOs) appear to counter Jenkins' simplistic categorization of Southern Christianity as conservative, apocalyptic, and supernatural. For example, four major Christian humanitarian NGOs in South Korea (World Vision Korea, Korea Food for the Hungry International, Good Neighbors International, Korea Compassion International) demonstrate that the majority of their humanitarian operations (eradicating poverty, promoting human rights, combating diseases, empowering women, and helping grassroots leadership groups) are almost identical with their Western counterparts. In this, Jenkins' claim of the conservative, apocalyptic, and supernatural tendency of Southern Christianity can easily be criticized. However, Jenkins pinpoints one crucial matter that needs to be further discussed:

> Textbooks discuss the faith in Africa and Asia chiefly in highly negative ways, in the context of genocide, slavery, and imperialism, and the voices of autonomous Southern Christianity are rarely heard. . . . Thus, understanding the religion in its non-Western context is a prime necessity for anyone seeking to understand the emerging world.[5]

My project in this sense becomes an attempt to highlight some of "the voices of autonomous Southern Christianity" in order to better understand Christian practices of mission in a non-Western context.

---

4. Ibid., 151–52.
5. Ibid., 215.

Another theoretical influence comes from Lamin Sanneh, professor of World Christianity at Yale University. Sanneh underscores two major themes as regards World Christianity: vernacularization by local agency through translation and the indigenous discovery of Christianity. First, Sanneh examines cases from Africa including Nigeria and Zambia in order to claim that a translatability of Christianity into the vernacular by indigenous agency is a secret of its success.[6] He supports the importance of local agency by showing the steady progress of Christianity in Africa distinctively after the withdrawal of the colonial power. By doing so, Sanneh highlights the indigenous response and local appropriation instead of missionary transmission and direction. Moreover, Sanneh puts an emphasis on the indigenous discovery of Christianity rather than missionary projects.[7] In other words, Sanneh is primarily interested in empowering local agency and initiatives. For instance, he pinpoints that Bible translation opened doors for many Africans to avoid Western domestication as well as creating movements of renewal in Africa. In this, according to Sanneh, Christian expansion through mission has more to do with a God-centered historical consciousness, that is, God's manifestation through various cultures and languages. Sanneh's theoretical tools help me explore Korean Christianity and its missional nature in the following manner. Although Western Protestant missionaries' work in Korea since the late nineteenth century deserves certain respect, especially in conjunction with their unanimous use of the Nevius plan (the emphasis on self-sustaining Korean Christianity) as I later explain, it is important to remember that Korean local Christians were the very agents who made the Christian faith relevant to their own political and sociocultural contexts. One remarkable example is shown in Korean Christians' arduous work to translate the Scriptures into the Korean language, thus constructing grounds for autonomous Korean Christianity. As a result, Korean Christianity has grown in a marvelous way on account of the active participation of Korean individuals and communities. More important, Korean Christians now take up a similar role to what their Western counterparts played a century ago, transmitting the Christian faith into other places around the globe in both word and deed. However, without critical reflection, the rapidly increasing influence of Korean international mission could pose many potential concerns. For example,

6. Sanneh, *Translating the Message*.
7. Sanneh, *Whose Religion Is Christianity?* 10.

there is always the danger of imposing some aspects of Korean culture on locals that might disregard the indigenous context. In this regard, Korean Christian missionaries must bear in mind the multifaceted nature of world Christianity as Sanneh cautions:

> More languages are used in prayer, worship, and the reading of Scripture in world Christianity than in any other religion in the world ... in the West that fact is counterintuitive, for people think of Christianity not as a pluralist religion but as monocultural and unifocal ... Christianity is not intrinsically a religion of cultural uniformity, and it has demonstrated that empirically by reflecting the tremendous diversity and dynamism of the peoples of the world.[8]

Finally, Andrew Walls, one of the most respected scholars in Mission Studies, provides me with an important theoretical grounding in embarking on this project. Walls weighs in heavily on the concept of missionary movement throughout his work. He considers the missionary movement as the single most important development in modern Western Christianity—functioning as a connecting terminal between Western Christianity and Christianity in the non-Western world.[9] He explicates that the older missionary movement from the West (influenced by Pietism and Revivalism), which upheld such principles as the same faith, testimony, and responsibility, created the idea of the representative of the total Christian community.[10] As a consequence, the older missionary movement gave rise to a series of voluntary societies, which mostly operated based on a one-way traffic approach. In this, Walls brings out two critical implications. First, the territorial "from-to" idea that bolsters the older missionary movement has to be replaced by a new concept that appropriately addresses the emerging world Christianity. Second, the lack of an inter-subjective mindset in the previous missionary movement calls for a new paradigm for mission where a two-way traffic approach (sending and receiving or transmission and reception) can be actualized in the midst of fellowship, sharing, and reciprocity. In this, it is noteworthy that Walls considers the missionary movement from the West as "only a vital

---

8. Ibid., 84 and 130.
9. Walls, *Cross-Cultural Process*, 34.
10. Walls, *Missionary Movement*, 255.

episode," further acknowledging Korea and Brazil as some of the major missionary-sending centers of our time.[11]

In addition to the aforementioned theoretical reasons, I want to explain some of the practical, personal motivations that have propelled me to continue with this project. First of all, those who are interested in Korean Christian mission—Korean Christian humanitarian mission in particular—can easily notice the dearth of studies conducted in this area. In light of that, my undertaking of this project could potentially contribute to initiating further discourse related to the subject. Second, I want to challenge and trouble any type of simplistic categorizations regarding Korean Christianity and its global mission through this project, further complexifying the dynamics of Korean Christian mission. As I described above, some scholars often lean toward making broad claims concerning Christianity in the non-Western world as exemplified in Jenkins' statement on the supernatural and conservative Christianity in the global South. I find this dangerous considering the complex nature of individuals and their communities around the world. By highlighting some of the differing, multifaceted features of Korean Christian practices of humanitarian mission, I want to challenge any monolithic claim concerning this matter. Instead, I underscore the need to pay attention to the multiplicity of Korean Christian mission in general and Korean Christian humanitarian mission in particular. Finally, by examining Korean Christians' mission practices on the ground, I want readers to better grasp some of the important characteristics of Korean Christian humanitarian mission. While some academics have observed the rapidly increasing number of Christian missionaries from Korea, it is difficult to find a single study that aptly illustrates Korean missionaries' international mission enterprises in detail. In this regard, my project is unique and has potential to broaden the scope of discourse in Mission Studies, International NGO Studies, and World Christianity.

## METHODOLOGICAL APPROACHES

There are three important methodological groundings in undertaking this project. First, I aim to highlight some of the ways in which Korean NGO missionaries attempt to speak of God in public, potentially constructing a mutually critical correlation between their Christian faith and

---

11. Walls, *Cross-Cultural Process*, 45.

secular society.¹² In this, David Tracy's revisionist or critical correlation model sheds light on my methodological approach.¹³ Tracy highlights the significance of the correlation between Scripture, tradition, experience, and reason in a mutually critical manner.¹⁴ In other words, to Tracy, the Christian faith needs to interact with the society and culture which it is set in a reciprocal way. As I later elucidate, Korean NGO missionaries through their humanitarian mission attempt to make their faith public and relevant to what the global society promotes including improving health and educational systems, advocating human rights, and challenging poverty. Throughout my project, therefore, I examine ways in which this type of mutual correlation (i.e., between Korean Christianity and its historical, socio-cultural, political, economic, and theological surroundings) takes place in the context of Korean NGO missionaries' international development work.

My second methodological grounding has to do with the concept of praxis, theology in action. That is, theory and practice are inextricably joined, thus rendering theology as performative knowledge. In agreement with John Swinton's claim, I strongly believe practical theology has to be a reflective discipline that leads to a theology of action:

> Practical theology is fundamentally action research . . . presenting itself as a quite specific form of action research with a particular understanding of the nature and purpose of action; not simply as a way of gaining new knowledge, but also as a way of enabling new and transformative modes of action.¹⁵

This praxis-oriented methodology aptly explains some of the reasons why Korean NGO missionaries dedicate their lives to humanitarian mission dealing with human sufferings such as poverty, disease, and injustice.

Finally, I consider qualitative research as one of the most critical elements of my methodology. As a process of "careful, rigorous inquiry into aspects of the social world," qualitative research methods provide helpful, conceptual frameworks that can be practically useful.¹⁶ In this, I am neither in search of a set of neatly organized theories nor a systematic completeness that can generalize the complex world of Korean

12. Graham et al., *Theological Reflection*, 13.
13. Tracy, *Blessed Rage for Order*, 34.
14. Swinton and Mowat, *Practical Theology*, 77.
15. Ibid., 255.
16. Ibid., 31.

global mission or Korean humanitarian mission. Rather, in light of my two examples, Good Neighbors (GN) and Korea Food for the Hungry International (KFHI), I would like to describe their prominent historical, theological, and sociological characteristics as thoroughly as possible.[17]

In regards to my detailed research method, I employ three different approaches: namely, literary research, interview, and participatory observation. First of all, literary research becomes a crucial part of research particularly when I examine Korean Christian NGOs' public stances including their mission statements and theological foundation. In doing this, I analyze the two Korean NGOs' official websites that describe their theological and organizational identity combined with the study of related publications and news articles. Second, I use my interviews with some of the key members of the two Korean Christian NGOs, notably KFHI's CEO Dr. Chung Jung-Sup and GN's CEO Rev. Lee Il-Ha in order to clarify GN and KFHI's distinctive theological basis and development approach.[18] Finally, I include some of the findings from my previous research trips, especially the ones to Cameroon and Uganda. I do so to support some of the major arguments that I make in this project concerning Korean NGO missionaries' approaches to other faiths and their relationships with locals.

## KEY TERMINOLOGY

Throughout this book, there are several key, recurring terms that need to be further explained for the sake of argument. First of all, my use of the term "Korea" here points specifically to South Korea. I choose to do so primarily on account of its convenience and because I do not address issues pertinent to North Korea. Second, the meaning of the term "Korean Christians" in the book refers to Korean Protestant Christians. By doing so, I attempt to control the scope of this project by focusing on Protestant mission practices of Korean Christians. Thirdly, I prefer the term "mission" to "missions." Many Christians including missionaries tend to use two terms "mission" and "missions" interchangeably without particular

17. See Browning, *Fundamental Practical Theology*.

18. Korean names work differently than most Western names; that is, they begin with the last name followed by the first name, and most first names have two syllables. To minimize confusion throughout this book, therefore, I hyphenate all Korean first names (e.g., Chung Jung-Sup). In the main text I follow the way that most Koreans address their names. When it comes to footnotes and bibliography, however, I follow the Chicago manual to maintain consistency.

distinctions. However, the term "missions" refers to ecclesiastical activities undertaken exclusively by the church and is geared toward bringing the gospel to non-Christians.[19] On the other hand, the term "mission" highlights the central role of God in any missionary activity in the world, which is not necessarily confined within the boundaries of the church. Fourthly, one of the keywords in this book is "nongovernmental organizations (NGOs)" and I highlight Christian, humanitarian NGOs that generally undertake both international and domestic projects. However, since my research has more to do with the international realm of their work and most Christian humanitarian NGOs in Korea operate internationally, my use of the term NGOs specifically relates to international non-governmental organizations (INGOs). Finally, in utilizing the term "humanitarian," I want to explain some other related terms: international aid, relief, and development. The three terms have been widely used by a variety of international humanitarian NGOs (e.g., International Relief and Development, Catholic Relief Services, Lutheran World Relief, Christian Aid, World Jewish Relief, Islamic Relief Worldwide, etc.) and have often been used interchangeably without specific distinctions. Generally speaking, "international development" is a holistic term that encompasses a wide range of human development including poverty, education, governance, human rights, and it tends to promote and be associated with long-term, sustainable solutions to problems. In contrast, the other two terms, "disaster relief" and "humanitarian aid," tend to focus on short-term fixes that could alleviate urgent problems. On the other hand, however, it is noteworthy that some scholars and practitioners use the term "international aid" as an umbrella concept that overarches both "relief (short-term projects)" and "development (long-term programs)." Throughout this project, I choose the former approach, thus often using the phrase "humanitarian aid and development NGOs." This means that the term "humanitarian" here includes both short-term aid projects and long-term development programs. Nevertheless, I would like to emphasize that this book is mainly focused on the "international development" aspect of Korean Christian humanitarian NGOs.

## STRUCTURE

Korean Christian mission has rapidly changed over the past few decades. Its focus has become diverse ranging from "evangelical mission" to

---

19. Cardoza-Orlandi, *Mission*, 13.

"humanitarian mission," thus now addressing public interests. In fact, the humanitarian mission is multifaceted in terms of mission statement and development practice. To examine this multifaceted humanitarian mission, I explore three Korean organizations: Global Mission Society (GMS), Korea Food for the Hungry International (KFHI), and Good Neighbors (GN). Representing the growing popularity of non-governmental organizations (NGOs) among Koreans, KFHI and GN expand the spectrum of Christian mission and are differentiated from the predominantly evangelistic, ecclesiastical mission that I exemplify through GMS. Both KFHI and GN undertake similar development projects including child development, health, water, education, and food programs. However, there are many differences. Some of the differences include their public stance as regards mission statements and actual development practice. In terms of the public stance, KFHI emphasizes the holistic (e.g., physical and spiritual) dimension of human development within which evangelism is considered crucial. This is differentiated from GN's focus on improving the quality of human life while distancing itself from evangelism. When it comes to actual development practice, KFHI's church-centered development operations are different from GN's inclusive approach that embraces development partners regardless of their faith tradition. What does this tell us about Korean humanitarian Christian mission? To further this inquiry, I discuss some of the major implications including intercultural and interfaith dimensions of Korean Christian humanitarian NGOs, the sociology of religion, religion and development, their similarities and differences to American counterparts, and from "development or mission" to "development as mission."

In the first chapter, I offer a brief history of Christianity in Korea geared toward pinpointing the rise of Korean Christians' humanitarian, global mission. Korea not only epitomizes the rapid growth of Christian faith in the twentieth century, but also it exhibits a strong sense of missionary vocation, which propels thousands of missionaries to operate in every continent. However, the recent decline of Protestant church growth in Korea has begun to pose major challenges for many Korean Christians. It has become more so as the tradition of human liberation and socio-political reforms, deeply embedded in the history of Korean church, is threatened by materialistic capitalism as I later explain in light of recent arguments of several Korean scholars. This changing religious context in Korea combined with a variety of socio-cultural, economic, and political factors, therefore, calls for a new, relevant paradigm of contemporary mission. One notable phenomenon within the Korean mission then is its growing involvement in international aid and development. What becomes clear is that contemporary Korean Christian missionaries are somewhat different from their predecessors in the late 1970s as regards mission approaches. I explain this in light of Chun Ho-Jin's study that predicted the potential influence of Korean humanitarian mission. Furthermore, by using the outcomes of my interview with Kim Yong-Sung, a KFHI field staff officer in Uganda, I illustrate the changing mindset about Christian mission among Korean NGO missionaries—not simply to convert unbelievers for the sake of saving souls but to care for those in need through humanitarian mission inspired by the love of God manifest in Jesus Christ.

Chapter two introduces and explains major characteristics and development activities of KFHI and GN, two major international humanitarian NGOs in Korea. It includes the two organizations' brief history, statistical data (e.g., the number of employees, annual budget, etc.), Christian identity, mission statement, organizational style, and areas of aid and development operations. Furthermore, I juxtapose the humanitarian mission of KFHI and GN with the purely evangelistic, ecclesiastical mission of the Korean Presbyterian Global Mission Society (GMS), the largest denomination-based mission organization in Korea. By doing so, I lay out a spectrum of Korean Christian mission.

In chapter 3, I examine some of the historical implications of Korean Christian humanitarian mission. In the first section, I offer a brief, historical survey of Protestant humanitarian mission. It reveals that an element of humanitarianism has always been present in the ethos and practice of Protestant mission. The second section deals with a historical survey of the humanitarian dimension of Christian mission to and of Korea. Although many well-recognized Western missionaries who came to Korea at the dawn of the twentieth century were mostly evangelists and church planters, their initial evangelistic zeal was often accompanied by humanitarian mission. I illustrate this by reference to such missionaries as Horace Underwood, Mary Scranton, Horace Allen, and Bob Pierce. As Korean Christianity grew in numbers along with the economic development of Korea during the late twentieth century, however, the relationship between Western missionaries and Korean Christians changed from recipient/donor to partnership. What then are the concepts of mission that are important to Korean Christians? I claim that the meaning of mission for many Korean Christians has become increasingly diverse, ranging from purely evangelistic mission (saving souls) to faith-inspired, humanitarian mission. At the beginning, Korean missionaries felt the strong need to plant churches and evangelize people in other parts of the world in light of what Western missionaries had accomplished in Korea. However, as I further discuss, Korean Christians began to focus on the humanitarian aspect of global mission beginning in the early 1990s impacted by the rapidly changing socio-political, economic, and cultural atmospheres in and out of Korea. In the final section, I discuss the historical development in the diversifying of the theology of mission within Korean Christian humanitarian mission. I first observe two major themes in the theology of mission, namely evangelism and social action, which have been historically polarized and contended by many Western Christians. In further exploring this trend, I use Stephen Bevans and Roger Schroeder's work that discusses some of the historical backgrounds behind the contemporary polarization of Protestant mission theology. I examine the question: in what ways has the theology of mission in Korea developed over the past century? Despite the short history of Protestant Christianity in Korea, there have been a few theological streams that shaped the contours of Korean mission: for example, orthodox/evangelical and progressive/minjung theology. Most Korean Christians sided with the orthodox, evangelical camp, which underscored individual salvation and change while paying less attention to the importance of Christian social action compared to its progressive counterpart. However, the rise of Korean Christian humanitarian mission emerged in the early 1990s and since then the range of the theology of mission in Korea has been expanded. To demonstrate the diversifying mission theology of Korean Christianity, I examine three Korean Christian organizations: the evangelical mission theology of Korean Presbyterian Global Mission Society (GMS); the holistic, evangelical mission theology of KFHI; and the humanitarian mission theology of GN.

In chapter 4, I explore important themes related to the theology of mission and practical theology. This chapter includes three sections: the diversifying public mission theology of Korean Christian humanitarian NGOs, the influence of different theologies of mission—holistic evangelical, mainline Protestant, and Catholic—on Korean Christian humanitarian NGOs, and intercultural and interfaith dimensions of Korean Christian humanitarian NGOs. The first section develops my argument that Korean Christians have become interested in promoting the public, common good and in this process diverse public mission theologies emerge and impact their actual practices. In doing this, I briefly examine the contemporary development of public theology in order to locate KFHI and GN's mission theologies within the discourse. In the second section, I first examine three different mission theologies—Type A, Type B, and Type C—that have influenced evangelical, ecumenical (mainline Protestant), and Catholic Christians. Then I locate mission theologies—Christology, ecclesiology, and eschatology in particular—of Korean Christian humanitarian NGOs in juxtaposition with the three theological frameworks of mission. When it comes to Korean Christian humanitarian NGOs, the holistic-evangelical (with more emphasis on evangelism) and the mainline Protestant, Catholic (with more emphasis on faith-inspired humanitarian action) theologies of mission have become influential. In examining KFHI's theology of mission, I draw upon my participatory observations and interviews with KFHI missionaries in Kumi, Uganda. Also, in order to investigate GN's theology of mission, I use my interviews with its CEO, Rev. Lee Il-Ha alongside GN's public documents. In my third section, by drawing upon my observations of and interviews with Korean NGO missionaries, I argue that many Korean Christian humanitarian NGOs attempt to promote interculturality and most Korean expatriates tend to easily adapt to their host country's cultural environment and foster a sense of emotional solidarity in light of their own development experience. However, I also point out that there are some challenges as well including the exclusive "us and others" mentality that is often found among Korean NGO missionaries. In explaining the interfaith dimension of Korean Christian humanitarian NGOs, I argue that although promoting some type of interreligious relation has been challenging for Korean Christians because of the strong influence of conservative theological and cultural milieu of Korea, many Korean NGO missionaries have laid the groundwork for interreligious cooperation in the midst of working with communities of different faiths to varying degrees. Specifically, KFHI and GN's different approaches to people of other faiths show that the interreligious humanitarian partnership can be undertaken at various levels. In supporting this argument, I first explicate four distinctive Christian approaches to other faiths in conjunction with Race and Hedges' work: exclusivism, inclusivism, pluralism, and particularities. With this framework in hand, I locate KFHI's interfaith approach somewhere between exclusivism and inclusivism based on my field research from Yaounde, Cameroon and Kumi, Uganda. In terms of GN's interfaith approach, I find its similarities to inclusivism in the sense that GN attempts to embody the love of Christ without imposing a particular belief system on others. To substantiate this claim, I examine GN's recent public statement that clarifies its position on interfaith relations.

In my fifth chapter, I discuss the phenomenon of emerging Korean Christian humanitarian NGOs from various sociological perspectives. There are four sections: the growth of Korean Christian humanitarian NGOs and its socio-religious implications, religion and its role in international aid and development, similarities and differences between Korean Christian humanitarian NGOs and their American counterparts, and comprehensive community development of Korean NGO missionaries: a case study of KFHI's mission in Kumi, Uganda. The first section is based on the following premise: Christianity in Korea currently experiences a rapid transition, and while multilayered, this transition comprises two major shifts: internal and external. In terms of the internal shift, two subelements are prominent. On the one hand, its deeply missional nature rooted in conservative, traditional Christian values—epitomized in the evangelical fervor initially transmitted by Western missionaries—begins to face challenges which modernity has brought in its path. On the other hand, the gradually indigenizing Korean Christianity starts to recognize and reclaim its cultural roots and traits, which have been eclipsed by its Western missionaries' cultural supremacy in both implicit and explicit ways. When it comes to the external shift, the pervasive influence of globalization, secularization, and neoliberalism has to be addressed: that is, Korean Christianity is now at a crossroads in which it has to aptly deal with massive external impacts. As a result, it appears that Korean Christianity has come up with a variety of legitimating answers: at an internal level, holistic synthesis becomes one of the most striking features that represent Korean Christianity—e.g., the equal emphasis on both evangelism and social action, the conflating reality between Western utilitarian individualism and traditional Asian communal values. Also, at an external level, impacted by the globalization and secularization of the modern world, Korean Christianity promotes its public role in a de-privatizing manner catering to both religious and secular needs, while celebrating neoliberalism as an important factor that potentially boosts this cause. I believe that Korean international NGO mission represents one of the most quintessential ways in which Korean Christianity finds its niche in the midst of a tumultuous transition. In demonstrating this, I examine some of the relevant mission practices of KFHI and GN. The second section deals with religion and its role in international aid and development.

Specifically, I examine the current discourses (e.g., previous research, the historical background, ongoing arguments about dialogue and engagement of religion and development) concerning religion and development. This overview reveals that a significant amount of relationship has been established between religion and development over the past few decades at both academic and practical levels. I further explore some of the implications for Korean Christian humanitarian NGOs. I do so by answering two important questions related to GN and KFHI: What has been the relationship between religion and international development for Koreans and what lessons can they learn from the general discourse in religion and development? My third section explores similarities and differences between Korean and American Christian humanitarian NGOs. I claim that Korean Christian humanitarian NGOs, in comparison to their American counterparts, have revealed similarities including upholding of modern values such as efficiency and transparency, similar types of development operations, and the growing theological diversity related to organizational goals. There are also differences including Koreans' emphasis on hierarchical structures in contrast to Americans' strong belief in equal standing, and Koreans' valuing of group cohesion and harmony as opposed to Americans' individual autonomy. To demonstrate the similar diversity of characteristicsbetween Korean and American NGOs, I, on the one hand, point to KFHI and Samaritan's Purse (SP), which show the evangelistic penchant and, on the other hand, I draw upon GN and World Vision (WV), which focus heavily on the humanitarian motive. To do so, I examine the official websites and publications of Samaritan's Purse and World Vision along with my aforementioned interviews with the staff of the two Korean NGOs. In the final analysis, the term hybridity becomes a keyword that aptly describes the emerging characteristics of Korean Christian humanitarian NGOs. To explain the hybrid characteristics of Korean NGOs, I address the case of KFHI in which its valuing of financial transparency and performance-based hiring / promotion coexists with the unquestionable obeying of decisions made by those who are higher in rank and older in age. To support this argument, I interview several KFHI's staff in Seoul to find out in what ways they understand this hybrid dynamic. The fourth section offers a detailed description of Korean Christian humanitarian NGOs' mission practices. To do so, I focus on a group of KFHI missionaries in a rural town called Kumi, Uganda drawn from my research during the summer of 2008 and the fall of 2011. This section aims at demonstrating major characteristics of

Korean Christian humanitarian NGOs and the roles they play in terms of rural community development.

The final chapter takes on a critical inquiry—whether we can regard international aid and development as Christian mission particularly in the Korean context. In discussing this, I propose that the rise of Christian humanitarian NGO mission in Korea since the 1990s has widened the spectrum of Christian mission, further opening the possibility of redefining the relationship between development and mission, that is, from *development or mission* to *development as mission*. In other words, many contemporary Christians in Korea are able to see Christian mission as something multiple in its form. Also, the emerging Korean NGO mission opens a new arena in which development itself can be identified with Christian mission to varying degrees depending on how Korean NGO groups interpret and implement the concept of *development as mission* in their practices. In light of my interviews with the CEOs of KFHI and GN, I illustrate the changing trend of Korean Christian mission that now includes humanitarian aid and development to varying degrees.

# 1

# A Brief Historical Summary of Korean Christianity[1]

GLIMPSES OF KOREAN CHRISTIANITY IN THE SIXTEENTH AND SEVENTEENTH CENTURIES

THE HISTORY OF KOREAN Christianity began with Roman Catholic missionaries' work in Japan and China in an indirect way.[2] Gregorio de Cespedes (1551–1611), a Spanish Jesuit, was presumably the first Westerner to set foot in Korea. As a missionary in Japan, de Cespedes served as director of the Jesuit seminary in Osaka and later earned the great Toyotomi Hideyoshi's trust. When Hideyoshi invaded Korea in 1592, a well-known year for many Koreans for the heroic battle fought by Korean admiral Yi Sun-Shin, one of Hideyoshi's generals named Konishi happened to be a devout Christian alongside his many Christian brigade commanders and eighteen thousand men. When Seoul fell to the Japanese, one hostage, a little boy of noble birth, was taken to Japan and baptized under the name of Vincent, and he ended up becoming one of the early martyrs of Korea. De Cespedes, however, was not a missionary to Korea; rather we have very limited information about his time in Korea. Another landmark event has to do with the influence of Chinese Christianity. Matteo Ricci, who went to China in the late sixteenth century, became one of the most famous missionaries who joined the Christian

---

1. In writing my own brief history of Christianity in Korea, I primarily rely upon two major sources: Moffett, *A History of Christianity in Asia*; and Moreau, *Evangelical Dictionary of World Missions*.

2. Moffett, *History of Christianity in Asia*, 143.

mission in China. His adaptation to and respect of Chinese culture—such as his wearing of Confucian scholars' clothes—demonstrate his openness. It is noteworthy that one of his writings "True Meaning of the Lord of Heaven" reached Korea and was introduced by Yi Syu-Kwang in 1614. Also, the crown prince of Korea So-Hyun, who was sent to China as a hostage, later was befriended by a Jesuit missionary Johann Adam Schall von Bell[3] and accepted Christianity.[4] This could have become the impetus for a Catholic mission in Korea when Prince So-Hyun brought Chinese Catholics back to Korea. Unfortunately, he died after six days of his kingship in 1645. It took more than a century and a half for Korea, the hermit kingdom, to open up itself once again to be influenced by Chinese Christianity.

## THE UNIQUENESS OF KOREAN CHRISTIAN INITIATIVES IN CHRISTIAN HISTORY

What makes Korean Christianity unique has to do with the fact that Koreans themselves initiated the transmission of Christian faith by bringing it from China—first, by Roman Catholics in the late eighteenth century and later by Protestants in the late nineteenth century. Undoubtedly, Catholics dominated mission in Korea between the late eighteenth and almost all the nineteenth century. Lee Seung-Hun, a high-ranking ambassador's son, became the first baptized Korean Christian as a Confucian scholar. He was initially sent to China to continue the custom of the Korean kingdom—sending their representatives to the imperial court in Beijing as an act of respect. After being asked by three renowned Korean Confucian scholars—the Jung brothers—who were interested in the Christian religion and mathematics, Lee contacted Jean Joseph de Grammont[5] and was eventually baptized as the first Korean Christian in 1784. Upon his arrival in Korea, Lee began to baptize others including his close friend Lee Pyok. Korean Christianity then was carried out on a very intellectual level. For example, Jung Yak-Chong, who initially asked *Lee*

---

3. Johann Adam Schall von Bell (1592–1666), as a German Jesuit and astronomer, spent most of his life as a missionary in China, serving as an adviser to the Chinese emperor.

4. Prince So-Hyun, however, was not baptized, and he did not have an opportunity to initiate a bona-fide Korean Christianity due to his untimely death.

5. Jean Joseph de Grammont (1736–1812) was a French Jesuit missionary in China. De Grammont met Lee Seung-Hun in Beijing and later baptized Lee giving him the name Peter.

to acquire information about Christianity, was a Confucian philosopher and an author of *Principles of Christian Faith*. He was also a brother of Jung Yak-Yong, a nationally renowned Confucian scholar and advisor to the king. However, when Lee inquired from the Beijing missionaries about ancestor veneration, the Franciscan bishop de Gouvea did not permit it in light of what had happened to the Jesuit missionaries in China following "the Chinese Rites Controversy,"[6] which resulted in the temporary dissolution of the Jesuit mission in Beijing. The repercussions of Lee's inquiry concerning ancestor veneration were devastating. Many newly-converted Christians in Korea resisted Confucian rituals pertaining to ancestor veneration, and they experienced a series of persecutions by the pro-Chinese and culturally Confucian Korean government. For example, one of the first Catholic martyrs was Yun Ji-Chung who was executed in 1791 after he had destroyed his ancestor tablets.

## THE BEGINNING OF KOREAN CATHOLIC CHURCH IN 1792 AND PERSECUTIONS

Following the inception of Korean Christianity upon the baptism of Lee Seung-Hun, hundreds of Korean Christians were executed in the midst of numerous persecutions that lasted for decades. One of its first missionary martyrs was a Chinese missionary, Chou Wen-Mo, who in 1801 turned himself in after six years of mission in Korea in order to protect his Korean Christian friends. In this process, Kim Tae-Kon, a Korean priest, became the first Korean priest martyr. Under the regency of King Ko-Jong's father Heungseon Daewongun, Korea became extremely nationalistic and exclusive to other neighboring countries and many Korean Christians and missionaries became martyrs during this time period. But when King Ko-Jong took over the regime in 1873, things began to change. He opened ports and borders, signing treaties with other countries such as the United States (1882), the United Kingdom (1883), and France (1886). This establishment of formal, diplomatic relations with many Western countries soon resulted in the growing Protestant missionary presence in Korea. Dominated by Presbyterian and Methodist missionaries from

---

6. From the 1630s to the early eighteenth century, the Catholic Church experienced a dispute over the legitimacy of Chinese folk religious rites. Dominicans believed that Chinese folk religion should be considered idolatry, whereas Jesuits, such as Matteo Ricci in China and Roberto de Nobili in South India, adopted some forms of the receiving culture. Pope Clement XI decided in favor of the Dominicans and this led to the enormous decline of the Jesuits' mission in China.

the United States and Canada, the Protestant mission in Korea began to outgrow its Catholic counterpart in terms of its numbers and influence.

## PROTESTANT MISSION IN KOREA SINCE 1884

Beginning around the third quarter of the nineteenth century, British and American missionaries initially played a crucial role in disseminating Protestantism in Korea.[7] The year 1884 has to be one of the most pivotal years for many Korean Protestants as well as foreign missionaries. Thanks to King Ko-Jong who employed a comparatively tolerant policy toward foreign countries unlike his predecessor, Daewongun, now many doors for missionaries were flung open. Before 1884, there were few attempts to deliver the gospel and carry out Protestant mission in Korea such as those undertaken by Karl Guzlaff and Robert Thomas. Karl Gutzlaff, who had mostly worked in China, attempted to distribute Christian literature via China in around 1832. Later Gutzlaff translated the Lord's Prayer from Chinese to Korean as he temporarily stayed on an island off the west coast of Korea as an interpreter for a British trading vessel. In 1866, Robert Thomas, a Welsh Congregationalist, entered into Korea via the General Sherman, an American ship, but he and twenty two other men aboard were killed as the ship went into the river Daedong. With no concrete evidence available, many Korean Christians still believe that Thomas handed over a Chinese Bible to a Korean solider before he became a martyr.

Most importantly, similar to what happened to Catholics a century before, Korean Christians were the very agents who actively and intentionally propagated the Christian faith. For Catholics, it was Lee Seung-Hun who laid the groundwork; for Protestants, it was Suh Sang-Yun, a ginseng dealer. In 1873, Suh encountered John Ross and John McIntyre of the Scottish Presbyterian Mission while searching for ginseng around the border between Korea and China. After receiving and studying a copy of the Gospel of Luke translated into Korean by Korean merchant-translators, Suh became Christian and gathered a group of believers in the village of Sorai. This story illustrates that Korean Christianity was primarily initiated as "a self-evangelized church" with a strong focus on "the translation of the Bible into the Korean vernacular" and the Biblical literacy.[8] Then finally following the year 1884 numerous missionaries

---

7. Kang, *Christ and Caesar*, 8.
8. Park, "Korean Protestant," 59.

from the North Atlantic, including Presbyterians Horace Allen (1884), Horace Underwood (1885), Samuel A. Moffet, and Methodists Henry Appenzeller and the Scrantons, began arriving.[9] One noticeable phenomenon of many foreign missionaries in the late nineteenth and the early twentieth centuries has to do with their intentional efforts for unity. For example, Presbyterians and Methodists, the only Protestant denominations for the first six years of Protestant mission in Korea, agreed on the majority of their Korean mission strategies: for example, their emphasis on primary education, women's rights, translation of the Bible, and training of indigenous Korean leaders.

## THE NEVIUS PLAN AND THE REASONS FOR THE RAPID GROWTH OF KOREAN PROTESTANTISM

Most European and American Protestant missionaries in the late nineteenth century were impacted by a colonial or paternalistic mindset. R. Pierce Beaver, for example, explains the colonial mentality in his description of the late nineteenth century Christian mission strategies:

> Protestant missions changed greatly in their mentality and consequently in their strategy in the last quarter of the nineteenth century . . . mission executives and field missionaries, partially impacted by social Darwinism, took the colonialist view that Africans were inferior and therefore could not provide ministerial leadership; thus Europeans were needed to fill leadership positions.[10]

While the imperial, colonial influence of some Western missionaries needs to be critically viewed, one noteworthy event was their employing of the Nevius Plan, which emphasizes three crucial strategies for Christian mission: self-propagation, self-government, and self-support. The Nevius Plan was uniquely successful in Korea as the renowned Church historian Samuel Moffett highlights: "There is no dispute concerning the fact that the Korean church grew most rapidly in precisely those areas of the Korean peninsula where the Nevius Plan was practiced most faithfully."[11] More importantly, we have to remember that it was Korean local Christians who made the Christian faith relevant to their own political and socio-cultural contexts as Park Joon-Sik asserts: "The

9. Paik, *History of Protestant Mission in Korea*.
10. Winter and Hawthorne, *Perspectives*, 235.
11. Moffett, *Christians of Korea*, 61.

Nevius plan, which stressed the crucial importance of native leadership for church growth, became the universally accepted policy of Protestant mission in Korea, spurring the Korean church to be independent and self-supporting."[12] Thus, it appears that the secret of the vitality of the Korean church was clearly in accord with the independent spirit that the Nevius Plan intended in addition to other contributing factors such as Korean Christians' evangelistic passion, fervency in prayer, devotion to the Word of God in their native tongue, and indigenous leadership initiatives. However, one of the most influential factors for the growth and vitality of Korean Christianity had to do with its thirty-six years (1910–1945) of tragic colonial experience inflicted by Japan. The simple fact that more than half of the signatories of its symbolic declaration of independence in 1919 were Protestant Christians signifies the correlation between Korean nationalism and the later popularity of Korean Christianity. Also, the fact that many early Protestants were influential, charismatic leaders such as South Korea's first appointed President Yi Seung-Man (Harvard and Princeton University graduate and Methodist elder) and Yun Tchi-Ho (Emory and Vanderbilt University graduate later establishing academic institutions in Korea) might have impacted the growth of Christianity in Korea.

## THE REMARKABLE GROWTH OF KOREAN CHRISTIANITY IN THE TWENTIETH CENTURY

Since the inception of Protestantism in 1884, Korean Christianity has experienced explosive church growth, one of the most dynamic examples of rapid church growth in the world.[13] The Protestant population in Korea increased from 1.4 percent in 1920 to almost 20 percent in 1995.[14] Currently, there are more than fifteen million Protestant Christians and about forty-seven thousand churches in South Korea.[15] Why did such a rapid Protestant church growth take place in Korea? In exploring this question, I examine several contributing factors in line with Park Joon-Sik's analytical framework.[16]

---

12. Park, "Korean Protestant," 59.
13. Jung, "Renewing the Church for Mission," 237.
14. Ibid., 238.
15. Tennent, *Invitation to World Missions*, 315.
16. Park, "Korean Protestant," 59–61.

## a) Geopolitical and Historical Factors

Some of the crucial backdrops concerning the impressive growth of Protestantism have to do with Korea's unique historical and geopolitical situations. Above all, the Japanese annexation and colonization of Korea between 1910 and 1945 left an indelible scar on the Korean psyche. Devastated by the loss of independence during the time period, Koreans sought ways to promote Korean nationalism and embraced Christianity as "a viable channel for expressing its nationalistic sentiment against the Japanese."[17] Thus the life of Protestant churches was inextricably linked to the spirit of "nationalism, political resistance, and democracy" from its inception."[18] Korean Christians' relentless commitment to Korean nationalism and independence, however, often ran counter to the overall mission strategies of Western missionaries who adhered to their political neutrality.[19] Ultimately, the incessant efforts of Korean Christians paid off and Korean Christianity gained its rightful place as "a legitimate religion of Korea."[20] Similarly, Kim Byong-Suh, emeritus professor of sociology at Ewha Woman's University in Seoul, offers important insights in relation to historical and geopolitical factors. Kim explains that the major reason why the Korean Protestant church outgrew its Catholic and Buddhist counterparts in Korea had to do with its long tradition of advocating human liberation.[21] For instance, during the final years of the Chosen dynasty, it was church leaders who attempted to reform the feudalistic nation and later fearlessly fought for independence from Japanese colonization. After the independence of Korea, many Protestant organizations (National Council of Churches, Urban Industrial Mission, YMCA, etc.) continued this spirit of human liberation through their human rights activities, thus gaining a great amount of respect, credibility, and support among a wide range of people in Korea. The popularity of some churches in the 1970s, to a lesser extent, resulted from their engagement in struggling for democratic rights against military regimes coupled with nationalist causes—by suffering with their minjung, the socio-politically and economically marginalized. The churches' unwavering advocacy for democratic reform was finally actualized in 1992 when the country had

---

17. Son, *Korean Churches*, 14.
18. Suh, "American Missionaries," 9.
19. Nahm, *Korea under Japanese*, 193–219.
20. Lee, "Political Factor," 120.
21. Buswell and Lee, *Christianity in Korea*, 324.

free elections. Then in 1997, Kim Young Sam—a Presbyterian elder—became the first democratically elected civilian president of the Republic of Korea.

## b) Socio-cultural Factors

Confucianism has permeated deeply into the Korean society and culture since the fifth century, and during the Chosen Dynasty (1392–1910) Korea successfully established "the most Confucian society in East Asia."[22] One notable aspect is that a great deal of Confucian values did not conflict with those of Christianity; on the contrary, they showed many affinities and engendered "dynamics of complementarity rather than of confrontation."[23] For example, Western missionaries' arduous promotion of "modern education" and "strict moral teaching" were in accord with Confucianism's "reverence for learning" and "austere moral mode."[24] As a result, the striking socio-cultural similarities between Christianity and Confucianism provided an optimal environment for church growth.

## c) Religious Factors

Another important factor concerning the rapid growth of Korean Christianity hinges on the suitable religious atmosphere into which Christianity was able to assimilate in a relatively easy way. David Chung, for example, explains that "the religious tradition of Korea had in a substantial way such congenial elements as the monotheistic concept of God, longing for salvation, messianic hope, and eternal life."[25] In a similar vein, Samuel Moffett argues:

> Christianity did not deny much that people had loved in the old beliefs. Like Confucianism, it taught righteousness and revered learning; like Buddhism, it sought purity and promised a future life; like shamanists, Christians believed in answered prayers and miracles.[26]

In sum, Korean Christians, due to the similarities between their traditional religions and Christianity, were able to accept the new faith

22. Park, "Korean Protestant," 59.
23. Grayson, *Korea*, 76.
24. Park, "Korean Protestant," 59.
25. Chung, *Syncretism*, 179.
26. Moffett, *Christians of Korea*, 82–83.

without extreme conflicts. Shamanism, for example, is one of the most salient traditional Korean religious belief systems that has influenced Korean Christianity. Despite its deep historical roots in Korea, shamanism has been considered "superstitious, anti-modern, and even demonic" by modern Koreans in general and Korean Protestants in particular.[27] Although Korean shamanism has not necessarily been in a congenial relationship with Korean Protestants, its widespread influence on Korean culture appears to be hard to deny, often providing a form of religious practice from which Korean Protestants have adopted.[28] One good example is the spiritual implication of mountains for Korean shamans that runs in parallel with the popular Protestant practice of mountain prayers. Korean shamans have always emphasized the important locus of mountains:

> Shamans described some mountains as *wild, uninhabited, magical* spaces where the gods' force was strongest and the shamans' visions the most vivid. Shamans visited mountains with clients to periodically recharge their own inspirational batteries.[29]

Moreover, Korean shamanism has transformed itself in such a way that "gods, ancestors, and skillfully inspired shamans have adroitly managed to move with modernity," thus catering to the needs of modern Koreans who live in a highly capitalistic and industrialized world.[30] In this process, Korean shamanism is often identified and valued as a Korean cultural tradition that has more to do with arts and entertainment than religious or spiritual practice:

> Korean shamans claim new respect as a national icon . . . Koreans regardless of religion or background can enjoy performances of *kut*—a ritual in which Korean shamans interact with gods and ancestors by doing a variety of small rituals to placate them and sustain their favor—and even join in ecstatic dancing at the end, so long as the spiritual content of these events is glossed as a cultural entertainment.[31]

More importantly, Korean shamanism centers upon this-worldly blessings such as material wealth and good health. During Korea's

27. Kendall, *Shamans*, introduction xx and 32.
28. See Kim, *Korean Religious Culture*.
29. Kendall, *Shamans*, 184.
30. Ibid., 205.
31. Ibid., 32.

industrial process, represented by Saemaeul Undong (the New Community Movement)[32] of President Park Jung-Hee (1963–1979), Koreans looked for a place where they could pursue this-worldly blessings and many Protestant churches catered to this need. One good example is Rev. Cho Yong-Gi at Yoido Full Gospel Church in Seoul whose message has been based on three beats blessings—the blessings of health, material prosperity and going to heaven upon death.

*d) Economic Factors*

The rapid economic development of Korea since the 1960s has surprised the world, and Korea is often referred as one of "the Four Asian Tigers or Asian Dragons." It is noteworthy that the most dramatic church growth in Korea concurrently occurred around urban centers during its period of rapid industrialization and economic development, a tenfold increase of Protestant membership between 1960 and 1980.[33] In explaining this interesting correlation, Park Joon-Sik comes to the following conclusion:

> Seeking to alleviate their enormous physical and emotional dislocation and alienation, and searching for an alternative community to the close-knit rural social networks, many Koreans turned to churches . . . the churches helped sustain the moral and spiritual values of the nation in the midst of country's rapid economic transition.[34]

The Korean churches then provided supportive moral and spiritual havens for many Koreans who were experiencing enormous pressures exerted upon them by the "radical social and economic changes."[35]

Alongside the aforementioned reasons, there are also several spiritual factors for the explosive growth of the Korean church: "strength of the local church by Spirit-filled and hard-working pastors; strong emphasis on prayer through daily early dawn prayer meetings, all night prayer meetings, and prayer mountains for spiritual renewal; grassroots evangelism; well-organized cell-group Bible study; abundant supply of Christian workers through theological education; faithful stewardship

---

32. Saemaeul Undong was a national initiative for rural economic development launched in 1970 by President Park.
33. Buswell and Lee, *Christianity in Korea*, 323.
34. Park, "Korean Protestant," 59.
35. Roberts, *Religion*, 85.

in tithes; and personal service for the church."³⁶ As a consequence, the mushrooming of mega churches has become a symbol of Korean Protestant Christianity.

While the impressive growth of Korean churches deserves our full attention, some of the recent statistical reports on Korean Protestant Christianity show a declining or maturing trend of its previously dramatic growth. Park Joon-Sik, for example, notes the decreasing percentage of Korean Protestant population between 1995 and 2005, from 19.7 percent to 18.1 percent, in light of the data collected from the Population and Housing Census Report in Korea.³⁷ Park juxtaposes the decreasing growth rate of Korean Protestantism with the preceding tenfold growth that took place between the 1960s (623,000) and the 1980s (6,489,000). Interestingly, it appears that the precisely same factors that contributed to the phenomenal growth of Korean Christianity until the early 1990s caused it to lose impact on the Korean society over the following decade.³⁸ First, I discussed that Korean Christianity earned its reputation as a legitimate Korean religion through relentless involvement in nationalistic, liberation-related activities during the Japanese colonial period. However, since Korea became independent, Korean Protestant churches gradually began to adopt generally pro-government tendencies, particularly during the 1970s and 1980s under dictatorial, military regimes. Instead of advancing democracy and advocating for the oppressed, the majority of churches acquiesced countless violations in human rights perpetrated by the military regimes, therefore losing their trust and credibility among the Korean public. Ironically, however, the generally pro-government approach of Korean Protestant churches during this era led to massive numerical growth. It was perhaps because this conservative approach unfortunately appealed to many Koreans who were desperately seeking security, education, and upward mobility under the protection of their military government. At the same time, this seems to become one of the reasons why the numerical growth of Korean Protestantism began to stall from the early 1990s when Korea became a civilian-led, democratic society. Secondly, Korean churches have lost their interest in influencing the Korean society and culture while enjoying rapid growth.³⁹ In other

---

36. Moreau, *Evangelical Dictionary*, 546.
37. Park, "Korean Protestant," 60.
38. Ibid., 61.
39. Grayson, *Korea*, 169.

words, they have ignored the critical mission of the Church: "the steady, relentless turning of all the mental and moral processes [of society and culture] toward Christ."[40] For example, Korean Christianity continues to support a Confucian value of strictly hierarchical relationships, thus perpetuating "social stratification among its members"[41] and neglecting the socially marginalized.[42] Finally, the religious factor, namely the influence of shamanism, seems to have affected the declining trend of Korean churches in relation to economic, material prosperity.[43] Korean Protestants' strong proclivity toward this-worldly, material blessings, for example, seems to have produced a large number of nominal Christians. The following statistics indicate the possibility that many of them have become disenchanted by Korean Protestantism and decided to leave the Protestant tradition:

> Among those who changed their religion, 45.5 percent had once belonged to a Protestant church, in comparison to 34.4 percent who had left Buddhism, and only 14.9 percent who had left Catholicism. Protestantism is the religion least likely to be considered for adoption by those without religious affiliation.[44]

It also alludes to the possibility that Korean Protestantism might have lost sight of the sacrificial, humbling aspect of Christian discipleship while being preoccupied with worldly causes. This discouraging trend has coincided with the fact that the middle class now makes up the majority of Korean Christians.[45] If Korean Christianity wants to reclaim its trust and credibility among the public, it will have to engage actively in the lives of the suffering, poor, and marginalized.[46] That is, instead of being preoccupied with numerical growth and materialistic expansion, Korean Christians need to foster a type of transformative mission, which concerns itself about sufferings and hopes of not only Koreans but also the global community.

---

40. Walls, "Mission of the Church," 21.
41. Park, "Korean Protestant," 61.
42. Buswell and Lee, *Christianity in Korea*, 360, 366–67.
43. Gwak and Hendriks, "Interpretation," 62.
44. Park, "Korean Protestant," 61.
45. Hong, "Revisiting Church," 191.
46. Costas, *Liberating News*, 31.

## THE RISE OF KOREAN WORLD MISSION SINCE THE LATE TWENTIETH CENTURY

Korea has become one of the most important mission centers in the world especially since the 1970s spurred by its rapid economic growth, political stability, and modernization.[47] The rapid increase in numbers of Korean Christians certainly shocked the world and its missional nature is truly remarkable. One source reports that the number of Korean missionaries has grown from ninety-three (1979) to about twenty thousand (2009) with two hundred and seventeen mission organizations in one hundred and eighty countries.[48] By utilizing its widespread connections around the globe through the Korean diaspora, Korean Christianity has become one of the most influential mission networks of our time.[49] In the process, it has established a wide spectrum of mission organizations geared toward church planting, education, medical services, leadership training, international aid and development. Therefore, the very cross-cultural diffusion that took place in Korea less than a century ago has quickly created multiple missionary, cross-cultural initiatives. In sum, Korea not only epitomizes the rapid growth of Christian faith in the twentieth century, but it also exhibits a strong sense of missionary vocation, which propels thousands of missionaries to operate in every continent.[50] However, the recent decline in Protestant church growth in Korea has begun to pose serious challenges for many Korean Christians.[51] It has become more so as the tradition of human liberation and socio-political reforms, deeply embedded in the history of Korean church, is threatened by materialistic capitalism.[52] The decreasing growth rate of the Korean missionary movement in recent years then seems to become one of the results. For example, Moon Sang-Cheol, executive director of the Korea Research Institute for Mission in Seoul, notes that between 2008 and 2011 there was "a growth of only 1,338 (from 18,035 to 19,373)" for Korean foreign missionaries and "the number of mission agencies has decreased from 190 to 168 due to closures, mergers, and inactivity."[53] Over the recent years,

---

47. Tennent, *Invitation*, 315.
48. See Kang, "Basic Missionary," 29–40; Johnson and Ross, *Atlas*, 259–69.
49. Kim and Ma, *Korean Diaspora*, 135.
50. Walls and Ross, *Mission*, 2.
51. Buswell and Lee, *Christianity in Korea*, 310.
52. Ibid., 327–28.
53. Moon, "Missions," 84.

there has been growing criticism among Korean Christians of some of the negative impacts of Korean overseas mission including their lack of interest in "infrastructure development, strategy for field ministries, care of missionary families, leadership development, crisis management, and preparation for missionary retirement."[54] One notable example relates to the "numerical goal-setting in mission" that has potentially hindered the Korean mission from growing in terms of "the quality of missionary work."[55] As an alternative, those critics propose a biblical approach of "incarnational humility" in which Christian missionary's unconditional, non-numerical, compassionate love for specific people becomes the impetus for mission.[56] The changing contexts in Korea, therefore, demand a new, relevant paradigm of contemporary mission. One notable shift within Korean mission then is its growing involvement in international aid and development. Disenchanted by bureaucratic, institutional churches that pay less attention to global issues such as poverty, disease, and illiteracy while constructing more church buildings, many Korean Christians now have turned to transnational faith-based organizations with the hope to make their faith relevant to public life. What is becoming clear is that contemporary Korean Christian missionaries are somewhat different from their predecessors in the late 1970s as regards mission approaches. In the early stage of Korean foreign mission, the main objective of undertaking Christian mission was to convert unbelievers and save souls by building churches and training Christian leaders. Chun Ho-Jin, former Dean of Asia United Theological University in Korea, discusses some of the primary goals and direction of Korean foreign mission from the late 1970s until the early 1990s:

> Korean mission has been focused on evangelism and church building, which are reflective of the strong evangelistic inclination of Korean Christians . . . but the numbers and influence of those who are engaged in a type of humanitarian services—such as medical and development mission—are likely to grow.[57]

It is interesting that twenty years after Chun wrote the article, his prediction about the growing influence of Korean humanitarian mission appears to be valid. There are currently thousands of Korean missionaries

54. Bonk, *Accountability*, 181–83.
55. Moon, "Missions," 84.
56. Bonk, "Mission by the Numbers," 2.
57. Chun, "Current Issues," 3.

involved in humanitarian mission, which includes medical mission, education, disease prevention, disaster relief, food distribution, microfinance, agricultural development, etc.

The changing mindset about mission among Korean Christians is illustrated in the life and work of Kim Yong-Sung, who serves as director of International Development Institute (IDI) in Kumi, Uganda through KFHI. Kim is originally from South Korea and an elder at Saesoon Presbyterian Church in Seoul, which happens to be my home church. Kim has always been committed to ministry and the mission of Christian churches since his youth. However, Kim mentioned that his profession as a Korean army officer usually did not give him enough opportunities to bear witness to his faith. Later, Kim was increasingly influenced by Dr. Chung Jung-Sup, President of KFHI and also a highly respected, senior elder at Saesoon Presbyterian Church. Following his retirement from the Korean Army in 2008, Kim and his wife Suh Young-Soon went to Uganda. Prior to their departure, Kim and Suh completed a three-month long staff training with KFHI and officially became its overseas staff member. It was Dr. Chung who first urged Kim and Suh to go and serve in Kumi, Uganda. After much prayer and research, Kim and Suh agreed to leave for Uganda. They initially pledged a three-year long commitment but have recently decided to extend their mission for another three years. Since Kim is a close friend of my family and has known me for more than twenty years, he wholeheartedly supported my work with and research on KFHI. During the fall of 2011, I conducted interviews with Kim while studying the rural community development of Korean missionaries in Kumi, Uganda and teaching courses in theology at Kumi University.[58] One of the questions that I asked Kim was concerned with his understanding of Christian mission. As a response, he answered the following:

> I think that Christian mission must entail both physical and spiritual elements. My hope is certainly to show Ugandans the love of God and to invite them to accept the gospel of Jesus Christ. But I believe it is wrong to ignore some of the structural and global problems—including hunger, diseases, and illiteracy—that call for urgent humanitarian services. I find my aid and development mission with Ugandan friends very meaningful. I,

---

58. Located in the northeastern region of Uganda, Kumi is one of the most socio-economically neglected areas in Uganda. See Nganda, "Corruption Endemic in Uganda."

along with Ugandan staff and volunteers, begin each day with a daily devotional asking God for guidance and wisdom. Then we undertake a variety of mission programs such as distributing mosquito bed nets to locals, providing school supplies for children, and drilling and repairing wells and boreholes.

Kim's answer demonstrates one of the most remarkable, emerging trends within Korean mission. In other words, more and more Korean Christians and missionaries have begun to acknowledge that mission is not simply to convert unbelievers for the sake of soul-saving but also to care for those in need through humanitarian involvement.

# 2

## Introducing Three Korean Organizations
Global Mission Society (GMS), Korea Food for the Hungry International (KFHI) and Good Neighbors (GN)

To explore the emerging international, humanitarian activities of Korean Christian mission, I turn to two particular Korean NGOs whose development work has been widely recognized in Korea. Before introducing the two organizations, however, I begin this chapter by presenting an influential mission organization in Korea called Global Mission Society (GMS). GMS employs much more evangelistic and ecclesiastical mission strategies than KFHI and GN. In other words, the central mission of GMS is to spread the gospel to all nations by building churches and mobilizing local Christians. This evangelistic, ecclesiastical approach is still the predominant way for many Korean missionaries who undertake mission. By presenting the mission of GMS along with that of KFHI and GN, I aim at highlighting a full spectrum of Korean Christian mission. This chapter first examines the general background of each organization including a brief history, mission statement, and types of mission operations engaged in. It then discusses my own relationship with each organization and explains reasons why I decided to study these Korean Christian NGOs.

## GLOBAL MISSION SOCIETY

As the largest denominational mission agency in Korea, the Korean Presbyterian Global Mission Society (GMS) trains, sends, and supports more than two thousand Korean missionaries in over a hundred countries.[1] It was founded in 1998 as a new overseas mission department of the General Assembly of the Presbyterian Church in Korea (GAPCK). It also partners with educational and theological institutions, including Chong-Shin Presbyterian Seminary. The following faith statement of GMS shows that it strongly upholds the Presbyterian identity in undertaking global mission:

> We believe that the Bible is the Word of God inspired by the Holy Spirit. We take the Westminster Confession and Catechism as foundation of the reformed faith, and we follow the Constitution and Credo of the Presbyterian Church as standard of Church government.[2]

It is notable that GMS missionaries are required to acknowledge the Presbyterian faith. Furthermore, the ministry of GMS is largely two-fold: that is, church ministry (e.g., evangelism, discipleship, training pastors and lay leaders) and community ministry (e.g., education, medical mission, skills and job training). Despite its involvement in humanitarian services, the focal points of GMS' mission are evangelism and Christian discipleship through local churches. For example, GMS highlights four components in terms of its mission strategies: focusing on unreached peoples, concentration on strategic fields, team ministry, and mobilization of churches:

> We help missionaries focus on unreached people groups and maximize their opportunities to share the Gospel with those who have yet to hear it. . . . We recognize strategic fields and concentrate both manpower and material support on them. . . . The dynamic core of concentrating on strategic fields is the strengthening of team ministry among GMS missionaries and recognition of the need for partnership with other missions agencies . . . GMS helps mobilize churches and get them effectively involved in mission work both in developing material support and raising manpower.[3]

The above statement aptly demonstrates GMS' clear inclination to evangelistic mission. Also, GMS' ecclesiastical mission approach is indicated in its report in January 2012, which revealed that out of its 2,151 overseas

1. Global Mission Society, GMS Works.
2. Ibid.
3. Ibid.

Korean missionaries 1,972 were ordained Presbyterian clergy and their spouses.[4] In sum, the evangelistic, ecclesiastical mission of GMS represents one of the most commonly practiced ways in which Korean Christians engage in global mission.

My research on Korean humanitarian mission often took me to places in which GMS undertakes its global mission. For example, while visiting KFHI and GN missionaries in Ivory Coast (2008), Tanzania (2010), Uganda (2008, 2011), and Panama (2012), I also had opportunities to meet with GMS missionaries. Similar to KFHI and GN, GMS missionaries have strong Christian faith that motivates them to engage in global mission. However, unlike the other two humanitarian NGOs, GMS missionaries are predominantly involved in evangelism, church planting, theological education, and Christian discipleship. For example, in Abidjan, Ivory Coast, I met a GMS missionary who has been deeply committed to evangelistic mission. To do so, he established a small Presbyterian seminary geared toward training local pastors and church leaders. I met a GMS missionary couple, Rev. Lee and Mrs. Lee, in Morogoro, Tanzania in 2010. Fluent in Swahili, they have spent almost two decades planting churches and training local pastors. Rev. and Mrs. Lee currently serve at a local Christian high school in Morogoro as chaplains. In Kampala, Uganda, I interacted with five GMS missionary couples who have been engaged in theological education through Reformed Theological College (RTC). Particularly, Rev. Yoo Hyung-Ryul, as a founding member of RTC, has been involved with a variety of evangelistic missions. Since 1994, Rev. Yoo has helped hundreds of African pastors (including Ugandan, Rwandan, Sudanese, Congolese, and Kenyan) complete their theological education and further plant local churches. Finally, in Chiriqui, Panama, I got acquainted with a GMS missionary Woo Wong-Sup, who has provided pastoral ministry for the homeless and for people with substance abuse since 2005. Before Panama, Woo along with his Peruvian wife Sherly Tardio planted churches in Lima, Peru for more than ten years.

## KOREA FOOD FOR THE HUNGRY INTERNATIONAL

Korea Food for the Hungry International (KFHI) is currently the second largest international humanitarian organization from South Korea. Established in 1989, KFHI initially partnered with its Arizona-based

---

4. Ibid.

mother organization Food for the Hungry (FH), the American relief and development organization founded by Dr. Larry Ward in 1971. Inspired by Ps 146:7, which emphasizes the need to uphold the cause of the oppressed and to give food to the hungry, FH's mission is to walk with leaders, churches and families in overcoming all forms of human poverty by living in healthy relationship with God and his creation.[5] FH was registered in Geneva as FHI Association in 1982. However, in 2006, the FHI Association was reorganized into two independent entities—FHI Federation (FHIF) and FH Association (FH)—that share the same name, vision and, history of FHI Association. Since 2006, KFHI has become a member of Food for the Hungry International Federation (FHIF), which includes twelve national partners including Japan, Malaysia, Thailand, South Africa, Zimbabwe, and Costa Rica. Currently, KFHI operates in eighty countries with approximately thirteen hundred Korean field staff and twenty-three hundred local staff. The vision of KFHI is to respond to the call of God who encourages us to meet both physical and spiritual needs worldwide and it strongly affirms the vision of community (VOC) as its ultimate aim in any area of operation. VOC is geared toward mobilizing leaders, churches, and families of any given community in order to actualize self-sustaining community development that further affects and assists development initiatives of other communities. KFHI thus wants to advance one's God-given potential by: being equipped to satisfy the needs of people in a holistic manner; loving God faithfully; and reaching out to serve others. On a technical note, KFHI is a global partnership that focuses on poverty needs that relate to food and nutrition. It focuses on sustainable food production, water resource development, primary health care, and income enhancement. KFHI also assists in the areas of education, empowering indigenous organizations by working with local NGOs and churches, and implementing child development programs in order to improve the quality of life of needy children and their families—physically, spiritually, socially, mentally, and emotionally. Furthermore, it provides disaster and emergency relief.

Growing up in Seoul, Korea, I was very familiar with KFHI mostly because its former and current CEOs, Rev. Yoon Nam-Jung and Elder Chung Jung-Sup, were both leaders of my home church in Seoul, Saesoon Presbyterian Church. As self-professing evangelical Christians who also have been actively involved in the work of Campus Crusade for Christ,

---

5. Korea Food for the Hungry International.

they constantly introduced KFHI and its work to the congregation and in many cases they recruited church members for KFHI's international mission. Furthermore, I often heard about KFHI on radio and TV. I remember watching many short documentary programs on both Christian and national TV that introduced KFHI Korean expatriates who were serving in developing countries to Korean audiences. Those programs captured some of the tragic, desperate life circumstances (e.g., war, disease, famine, natural disaster) of those who live in impoverished countries and they tended to positively portray the selfless services of Koreans in a remote country. When the program was broadcast on a Christian cable such as Christian Broadcasting System (CBS) and Christian Television System (CTS), Korean expatriates were called missionaries and their evangelistic endeavor was accentuated. When their stories were told on a national channel such as Korea Broadcasting System (KBS) and Munhwa Broadcasting Company (MBC), however, their role as humanitarian workers was highlighted. Following my undergraduate degree in Korea, I came to the United States for graduate studies and ministerial training. It was almost a decade later that I began to look back on KFHI and its critical implications related to Christian mission. Few months before I was about to begin my doctoral work in Religion at Emory University, I had a chance to reunite with elder Chung, the current CEO of KFHI while I was visiting my family in Seoul. He explained to me how important his ministry with KFHI had been and urged me to join his upcoming trip to West and East Africa. I hesitated at first but later accepted his offer and went on a month-long journey to five different countries in Africa, visiting numerous KFHI projects sites and interviewing many KFHI missionaries and their local partners. Above all, the extensive involvement and unwavering passion of Korean Christian missionaries inspired and intrigued me during this time. Following the trip, I unofficially served KFHI as its international operations and development consultant. Then after completing KFHI's overseas staff training that took place in Tanzania during the summer of 2010, I was officially appointed as KFHI's international operations and development research advisor. More importantly, I have been privileged to conduct extensive research (between two weeks and four months at each location) in numerous developing countries in which KFHI missionaries undertake a variety of humanitarian programs.[6]

6. The list of countries I have visited and conducted research since 2008 is as follows: Cameroon (2008), Ivory Coast (2008), Burkina Faso (2008), Ethiopia (2008),

## GOOD NEIGHBORS

Established in 1991, Good Neighbors (GN) is currently the third largest international, humanitarian NGO that comes out of South Korea. Its founder Rev. Lee Il-Ha was a former employee of World Vision Korea with expertise in international aid and development. By utilizing his experiences with World Vision, Lee later founded GN, which was the first bona fide indigenous Korean aid and development agency. Although GN's organizational spirit is deeply influenced by the Biblical mandate to love God and to serve our neighbors, it neither encourages nor practices any types of proselytization. Thus, GN wants to differentiate itself from other Christian mission organizations that publicly practice evangelism. GN currently undertakes a wide range of relief and development projects around the world that challenge poverty, illiteracy, disease, natural disaster, social unrest, and human rights related injustice, etc. Headquartered in Seoul, GN's annual budget is over forty-two million dollars in support funds, drawn mainly from sponsorship dues, government subsidies, and donations. GN has close to twenty-five hundred domestic and international staff members and operates in twenty-five developing countries as of 2012. During my interview, Rev. Lee highlighted that he is very pleased with the enthusiastic support of the South Korean government alongside business corporations for his humanitarian enterprises. Also, he continued that one of his major life-long goals is to promote "the culture of giving" among Koreans. He was particularly proud of the fact that there are more than 330,000 regular donors and volunteers who work with GN. Similar to KFHI, GN mobilizes and partners with numerous Korean immigrant communities all around the globe. Since the majority of these Korean communities are centered upon Christian churches, there are many circumstances in which GN has to work with immigrant Korean Christians who understand the society and culture of the particular area. However, GN does not exclusively collaborate with Christian communities around the world. Rather it has promoted an inclusive approach that embraces aid and development partners of all backgrounds. As a result, GN's work has been internationally acknowledged by many secular international aid and development sectors. For example, United Nations Economic and Social Council (UN ECOSOC) granted GN General

---

Uganda (2008), Uzbekistan (2009), Mongolia (2010), Tanzania (2010), Peru (2010), Guatemala (2011), Mexico (2011), Kenya (2011), Rwanda (2011), Uganda (2011), and Panama (2012).

Consultative Status (GCS) in 1996, the highest status level for an NGO that is awarded to less than 4 percent of global NGOs. In addition, in 2007, GN was recognized by the United Nations with a Millennium Development Goal (MDG) Award for its achievements in universal primary education.

I first heard about GN approximately fifteen years ago when I was in college at Yonsei University in Seoul, Korea. Yonsei, as a private university that was established by American missionaries at the dawn of the twentieth century, required all students to attend its weekly chapel. Also, as a theology major, I had to attend a weekly chapel service specifically designed for seminary students. These were the occasions in which I had many opportunities to hear from Rev. Lee Il-Ha, Yonsei alumnus (with a degree in theology), who had represented one of the most influential humanitarian organizations in Korea. Lee shared with us a lot of heartbreaking and at the same time heartwarming stories that he and his overseas staff had experienced in the midst of serving the socially and economically marginalized both in and out of Korea. He then urged students at Yonsei to engage actively in such causes as eradicating global poverty and challenging injustices. Unfortunately though, I was not quite ready for his message back then; rather, I was overwhelmed with his message that focused on the enormity of physical sufferings that people in the developing countries experience. It was only when I began to study Korean Christian humanitarian NGOs in 2008 that GN and Rev. Lee came back to my mind. In order to learn more about the organization, I undertook my first research trip in 2010 and met with Rev. Lee. He was excited that I had become interested in global humanitarianism and shared a great deal of information with me during my interview. Furthermore, he introduced me to some of GN's top executives and put me in contact with Mr. Chang Chun-Yong, GN's public relations executive director, who has since then become my liaison with GN.

# 3

# History of Mission with a Special Focus on the History of the Humanitarian Dimension of Christian Mission with Respect to South Korea

HERE I WOULD LIKE to explore the broader mission historical context of the Korean Christian humanitarian mission within which the aforementioned two Korean humanitarian NGOs (KFHI and GN) operate. I begin with a brief historical account of Protestant humanitarian mission in order to set the stage for further discussion of Korean Christian humanitarian mission. It will then be followed by a historical survey of the humanitarian dimension of Christian mission to and of Korea, a centerpiece of the chapter. Finally, I explore the historical development of mission theology within Korean Christian humanitarian mission, which manifests a diversifying trend.

## A BRIEF SURVEY OF PROTESTANT HUMANITARIAN MISSION

The history of Protestant mission shows that its mission strategy has not been simply confined to evangelism; rather it has almost always coincided with humanitarian elements such as health and education. R. Pierce Beaver charts the humanitarian aspect of Protestant mission.[1] First, Protestants' world mission began in the early seventeenth century with the work of the chaplains of the Dutch Indies Company. It was later followed by the Puritans who engaged in New England mission to the American Indians around 1630. One crucial fact here is that major leaders among

---

1. Winter and Hawthorne, *Perspectives*, 231–38.

the Puritans, notably John Eliot and David Brainerd, focused on both evangelizing and civilizing Indian believers, which included education, skills training, and medical care. Thus, the civilizing mission elicited somewhat humanitarian aspects. Second, the first bona-fide sending mission from Europe was initiated by the Danish-Halle mission in 1705 when the King of Denmark commissioned German Lutheran missionaries to Tranquebar, a town located in the southeast of India. During this time, some of the pioneering leaders such as Bartholomew Ziegenbalg and Christian Frederick Schwartz adapted themselves to the local Indian culture and developed a mission strategy that included not only worship and preaching in the local Tamil language, but also education and medical programs. Furthermore, beginning in 1734, the Moravian missionaries, Count Zinzendorf and Bishop Spangenberg, were sent intentionally to some of the most socially neglected, disenfranchised people groups including slaves in the Danish-governed West Indies and promoted a mission strategy based upon self-support in the midst of communal living. Third, in the nineteenth century Protestant mission brought forth numerous mission strategies, mainly organized by members of mission societies including the Baptist Missionary Society (1792) in Britain and the American Board of Commissioners for Foreign Missions (1810). It is important to note that during this time missionaries rarely doubted the legitimacy of humanitarian mission. Rather, they promoted different types of humanitarian, civilizing mission that accompanied evangelism. One example comes from William Carey, an English missionary to India and a founder of the Baptist Missionary Society, who is often called "the Father of Modern Missions."[2] He asserts that "we are the subject of grace, and partakers of that spirit of universal benevolence and genuine philanthropy."[3] Although Carey's primary purpose in his missionary activity was to convert unbelievers to Christianity, his actual service in India included a broad spectrum of humanitarian enterprises. Carey and his colleagues, Joshua Marshman and William Ward, also known as the Serampore Trio, contributed to education, agriculture, technical expertise, and social justice, urging the colonial power to abolish inhumane cultural practices such as *suttee* (widow-burning), infanticide, and the maltreatment of lepers.[4] Another important mission strategy in the

2. Ibid., 282.
3. Ibid., 312.
4. Ibid., 261.

nineteenth century, the so-called "three-self" formula, relates to three individuals, Henry Venn (an Anglican of the Church Missionary Society in London), Rufus Anderson (a Congregationalist of the American Board of Commissioners for Foreign Missions), and John Nevius (an American Presbyterian missionary). By advocating the concept of self-governing, self-supporting, and self-propagating indigenous churches, they promoted the idea that local Christian leaders, instead of foreign missionaries, have to be the central agents for social transformation. Beaver, in this sense, summarizes that mission strategy of the nineteenth century included three main types of action—"evangelism, education, and medicine," geared toward "individual conversions, church planting, and social transformation."[5] Finally, the early twentieth-century mission was greatly influenced by the 1910 World Missionary Conference in Edinburgh. Following this conference, global church leaders started to acknowledge younger churches, giving them full authority and autonomy. Also, the Western mission societies and denominational boards began to adopt and promote mission methods that included a variety of humanitarian aid and development programs such as agricultural mission, urban industrial work, and rural community development.

In the final analysis, it becomes clear that the humanitarian aspect within Christian mission has always been closely connected to its mission strategy. This echoes what Paul Pierson describes in relation to the impact of Christian missionaries on social action and transformation:

> The Church of Jesus Christ has generally understood the transformation of society to be an essential part of its task . . . expectations of people obeying Christ has fueled hope that the culmination of this process of evangelization would bring about transformation of the social situations, the physical conditions and the spiritual lives of believers.[6]

In other words, almost all missionary movements in Protestant history have been concerned about a type of social transformation that entails care for the marginalized members of society through humanitarian services. At the same time, we need to reflect critically on the fact that missionaries often decided to support colonialism in order to accomplish their version of social transformation.

---

5. Ibid., 236.
6. Ibid., 279.

## A HISTORICAL SURVEY OF THE HUMANITARIAN DIMENSION OF CHRISTIAN MISSION TO AND OF KOREA

Many well-known Western missionaries who came to Korea at the dawn of the twentieth century were mostly evangelists and church planters. However, in many cases, their evangelistic zeal went hand in hand with humanitarian mission. For example, American missionaries Horace Underwood (Presbyterian) and Mary Scranton (Methodist) founded two of the most prestigious Universities in Korea, Yonsei University and Ewha Womans University.[7] Also, Horace Allen, an American medical doctor, was primarily involved in medical mission and then later became the first American ambassador to Korea. In a way, Western mission in Korea, alongside its strong evangelistic penchant, was usually closely connected to some type of humanitarian undertaking. It became especially so during the post-Korean War era when the war-torn Korean peninsula demanded a great deal of humanitarian aid. One quintessential mission agency was Rev. Bob Pierce's World Vision. Pierce was initially involved in Youth for Christ's evangelistic rallies in China in 1947. However, on his way back to the United States, he witnessed and became heartbroken by the desperate situation of war orphans in Korea. Following this eye-opening event, Pierce founded World Vision in order to help children orphaned during the Korean War. World Vision was certainly not the only mission organization that undertook humanitarian mission. Various denominational mission boards, led by Presbyterians and Methodists, desired to improve the quality of life in Korea although their ultimate goal was to work with Korean churches for evangelization. As Korean Christianity grew in influence and numbers along with the economic development of Korea during the late twentieth century, however, the relationship between Western missionaries and Korean Christians gradually shifted from recipient/donor to mutual partnership. The fact that World Vision Korea now contributes greatly to the World Vision International is living proof of the changing dynamics between the two. For example, Dr. Park Jong-Sam, the current CEO of World Vision Korea, proudly shared with me that his Korean branch has become one of the top five

---

7. Keller, *Spirituality*, 185. Mary Scranton chose the unconventional word "Womans" in order not to lump students together under the term "women," symbolizing that every female student at *Ewha* needs to be fully respected and cherished.

contributing partners among World Vision International's one hundred national headquarters.[8]

Korean Christian's strong inclination to mission is not a new subject. It has been introduced and recognized by numerous scholars including Philip Jenkins (2002), Andrew Walls (2008), and Dana Robert (2009). But not many have conducted a qualitative, detailed research in terms of the specificity and diversity of Korean global mission. What becomes necessary is to examine in what ways Korean Christians understand mission and how the perceptions and practices of mission have changed since its inception. What then are the concepts of mission that are important to Korean Christians? Briefly, I believe the meaning of mission has changed from being unidirectional to multidirectional, thus extending the spectrum of mission ranging from purely evangelistic mission (saving souls) to humanitarian mission. At the beginning, Korean missionaries' focus was exclusively on building churches and evangelizing the world. Similar to their Western counterparts, the Great Commission of Jesus Christ from the Gospel of Matt 28:18–20 was the basis of the Korean evangelistic mission. This biblical mandate of world evangelization was intertwined with the influence from Western missionaries. In other words, Korean Christians felt the need to evangelize people in other parts of the world in light of what Western missionaries had accomplished in Korea. However, as I later discuss, the changing global contexts in the late twentieth century called for and brought forth a new paradigm of mission for Korean Christians.

A historical development of the humanitarian mission of Korean Christians began with the changing political milieu both outside and within Korea. Externally, the collapse of the Berlin wall in 1989, together with the subsequent decline of communism, became the milestone event when it comes to undertaking Christian mission for many Koreans. For example, the increasing humanitarian need of the former Soviet countries opened doors for many Korean missionaries who had been eager to serve the physical needs of their neighbors and to spread the gospel in the previously communist countries. Internally, the Korean government began to promote internationalization, especially following its successful hosting of the Seoul Olympics in 1988. To usher in globalization, the Korean government declared the complete liberalization of overseas travel

---

8. I interviewed Dr. Park in the summer of 2010 at the national office of World Vision Korea in Seoul, Korea. The interview lasted for about two hours and we discussed a variety of issues.

for Korean citizens in 1989. Furthermore, the election of the first civilian president Kim Young-Sam in 1992 signaled the beginning of bona-fide democratization of Korea. Korea now, as alegitimate democratic state, hoped to actively engage in global affairs such as humanitarian involvement. It became more so in 2007 when Ban Ki-Moon, the former minister of foreign affairs in Korea, was elected as the Secretary General of the United Nations succeeding Kofi Annan. Since then, Ban has pressured his own South Korean government to be actively involved in international development assistance including the Millennium Development Goals (MDGs).[9] To accomplish this effectively, the Korean government has partnered with humanitarian NGOs in Korea such as KFHI and GN. In 2009, the Korean government announced that it will increase Official Development Assistance (ODA) from the current 0.1 percent of its Gross National Income (GNI) to 0.25 percent by 2015.[10] Strongly influenced by the changing external and internal dynamics in Korea, the characteristics of Korean mission began to become diverse. In other words, humanitarian mission has become an important part of Korean mission in addition to ecclesial, evangelistic mission, thus broadening the spectrum of Korean Christian mission. For example, Korea World Missions Association (KWMA)'s annual publication in 2010 hints at the changing dynamics of Korean mission. It indicates that the percentage of Korean Christian's humanitarian mission grew from almost zero in 1979 to about 20 percent in 2010.[11] One significant subject matter is types of mission theology upon which the Korean Christian humanitarian mission organizations are based.

## THE HISTORICAL DEVELOPMENT IN THE DIVERSIFYING OF THE THEOLOGY OF MISSION WITHIN KOREAN CHRISTIANITY

What is theology of mission? Many missiologists have attempted to define the term theology of mission. Evangelical Protestant scholars such as

---

9. Initiated by the United Nations in 2000, the MDG goals entail eight areas: (1) the eradication of extreme poverty and hunger; (2) universal primary education; (3) gender equality and women empowerment; (4) the reduction of child mortality rates; (5) maternal health improvement; (6) fighting diseases such as HIV and AIDS, and malaria; (7) environmental sustainability; and (8) global partnership for development.

10. According to the official OECD statistics in 2010, South Korea spent $1,168 million for development assistance (0.12 percent of its GNI).

11. *Korea World Missions Association Annual (KWMA) Publication*, 2010.

Craig Ott, Stephen Strauss, and Timothy Tennent, for instance, examine the task of missions that includes four salient motifs: (a) proclamation and conversion as the task of missions; (b) church planting and growth as the task of missions; (c) civilization and moral improvement as the task of missions; (d) philanthropy, humanization, and liberation as the task of missions.[12] Catholic scholars such as Stephen Bevans and Roger Schroeder prefer "a synthesis for prophetic dialogue" after presenting an overview of three salient strains concerning the theology of mission—(a) mission as participation in the work of the Trinity; (b) mission as witnessing to the justice of God's reign; (c) mission as proclaiming Christ as the only savior.[13] Having examined the previously explained definitions of theology of mission, one thing becomes clear. Two major themes in the theology of mission, evangelism and social action, have historically been polarized by many Western Christians, and the attempt to promote a type of holistic approach is a fairly recent development.

Stephen Bevans and Roger Schroeder, in *Constants in Context: A Theology of Mission for Today*, discuss some of the historical backgrounds behind the contemporary polarization of Protestant mission theology, especially in relation to the separation of evangelical Christians from the World Council of Churches (WCC) in the 1960s:

> The decade of the 1960s with its social and political turbulence was a time of transition and ferment for church and mission. While some Protestant and Orthodox Christians rejoiced over the potentiality of new life coming from the World Council of Churches (WCC), others felt less and less at home with these developments, to the point that Protestants would eventually distinguish themselves according to these differences and form two distinct Christian movements, each with its own theology of mission.[14]

One of the most controversial figures within the mission movement during the 1960s was Johannes Hoekendijk[15] who proposed progressive missiological views at the World's Student Christian Federation in Strasbourg in 1960. The major theme of Hoekendijk's argument, which strongly influenced the WCC during the sixties, was that the secular world, not

---

12. Tennent, *Encountering*, 106.
13. Bevans and Schroeder, *Constants*, 348.
14. Ibid., 260.
15. See Hoedemaker, "Legacy," 166–70.

the church, is the primary locus of God's mission.[16] Another important figure in the 1960s was Stephen Neill, a respected mission historian from Scotland, who asserted that "the age of missions is at an end and the age of mission has begun."[17] Neill hoped to recognize the growing churches in the non-Western world, which called for new perspectives on Christian mission: that is, God's mission is not geographically bounded and mission has to be undertaken on six continents by all churches.

Evangelical and conservative churches and their mission bodies, however, counteracted the progressive, ecumenical milieu of Christian mission represented by the WCC. For example, they held two major conferences in 1966, the Berlin Congress on Evangelism and the Wheaton Congress on the Christian World Mission, in order "to give wider visibility to the Evangelical movement"[18] and "to offer a biblically based alternative to ecumenism."[19] In the 1968 WCC Assembly in Uppsala, the divide between evangelicals and ecumenicals escalated when the conference resonated with what Hoekendijk had argued—the horizontal aspect of mission with more emphasis on humanization than salvation. In response, Donald McGavran, a Missiology Professor at Fuller Theological Seminary, wrote "Will Uppsala Betray the Two Billion?,"[20] attacking the liberal, ecumenical position on Christian mission within the WCC. Furthermore, in 1974, the Rev. Billy Graham sponsored the International Congress on World Evangelization at Lausanne, which "represented a high-water mark for evangelical identity and solidarity in mission and evangelism."[21] Led by John Stott, a highly regarded evangelical voice within the WCC, evangelicals then endorsed the Lausanne Covenant, which affirmed the authority of the Bible and the uniqueness and universality of Christ. Despite the fact that the Lausanne Covenant strongly espoused the primacy of evangelism and proclamation, it acknowledged social justice and evangelism as two crucial Christian duties. The quite surprising adoption of social justice was the outcome of arduous efforts undertaken by so-called radical evangelicals, mostly from the non-Western countries, including Rene Padilla, Orlando Costas, and Samuel

---

16. Bevans and Schroeder, *Constants*, 260.
17. Neill, *History*, 572.
18. Bevans and Schroeder, *Constants*, 260.
19. Scherer, *Gospel*, 167.
20. McGavran, "Will Uppsala," 1.
21. Scherer, *Gospel*, 167.

Escobar.[22] Fifteen years later in 1989, the Lausanne Committee for World Evangelization's (LCWE) second major missionary conference in Manila continued to carry on the spirit of the Lausanne Covenant. It produced a critical summary document called the *Manila Manifesto*, which not only reaffirmed the significance of proclamation but also included concern for the poor and interfaith dialogue, thus taking a more holistic approach.[23] Nevertheless, for many evangelicals, Donald McGavran's missiological model, the church growth movement, became prominent. Initially introduced in 1955 through his publication, *The Bridges of God*, church growth movement was based on the goal "to evangelize a whole people through people movement, the success of which can be demonstrated through statistical numerical growth."[24] McGavran's model was later modified by Ralph Winter, his colleague at Fuller, who stressed the importance of evangelizing "unreached peoples" through concrete information gathering.[25] Many evangelical churches, mission bodies, and parachurch organizations soon became avid proponents and agents of such mission theology.

Ecumenical or Conciliar movement in the twentieth century, which began with the milestone event—the Edinburgh Missionary Conference in 1910, became distinct following the 1968 Uppsala Assembly. Ecumenicals generally upheld Hoekendijk's progressive mission theology that underscored mission for the secular world. However, they soon faced considerable challenges from the secular world when the Kenyan leader John Gatu called for a moratorium on Western missionaries in 1971. Later at the Commission on World Mission and Evangelism (CWME) meeting in Bangkok (1973), ecumenical leaders declared "a call for liberation and an end of Western cultural and ecclesiastical dominance,"[26] thus signifying the transition toward "shared power and partnership between the Western and non-Western churches in the CWME."[27] Ecumenical leaders continued to wrestle with finding sound mission theology that could make Christian mission relevant to the secular world. In 1975 at the fifth assembly of the WCC in Nairobi, for example, they gathered to develop

22. Bevans and Schroeder, *Constants*, 261.
23. Yates, *Christian Mission*, 211.
24. Bevans and Schroeder, *Constants in Context*, 261.
25. Ibid., 262.
26. Ibid., 263.
27. Scherer, *Gospel*, 124.

ecumenical mission theology in an attempt "to reconcile churchly and worldly approaches to mission."[28] The 1980 CWME conference in Melbourne focused on the kingdom of God, which understood proclamation in a holistic sense—the dual emphasis on the church's critical role in undertaking social justice and evangelism. Then in 1982, the WCC Central Committee approved *Ecumenical Affirmation: Mission and Evangelism* within which the term mission is holistically defined.[29] One of the most controversial themes in the late twentieth century ecumenical mission theology was the relationship of Christianity to other religions. Among those who addressed the theme, Wilfred Cantwell Smith and John Hick were highly recognized. Smith, a missionary in India, claimed that God does not necessarily bring people to Christ but that believers of all religions can reach a fuller awareness of God through interactions with each other.[30] Hick proposed his pluralistic or relativistic theology, which urges Christians to shift from a Christocentric understanding of Christianity to a theocentric one.[31] Influenced by the ongoing discussion on interreligious relations, the WCC published *Guidelines on Dialogue with People of Living Faiths and Ideologies* in 1979. It considered interreligious dialogue as "a new way of ecumenical action and an expression of the Christian's approach to a wide range of activities of witness, service, and community relationship in a pluralistic world."[32] One of the most influential ecumenical mission theologians and practitioners in the late twentieth century was Lesslie Newbigin, a Church of Scotland missionary in India and bishop in the Church of South India. Newbigin asserted the emerging need for the church to appropriately deliver the gospel to the post-Christian West.[33] Newbigin established in 1982 the "Gospel and Our Culture" program in order to understand "a missionary encounter with post-Enlightenment culture in the West."[34]

In what ways has the theology of mission in Korea developed over the past century? Despite its short history, Korean Protestant mission has been shaped by a few theological streams such as orthodox/

28. Ibid., 126.
29. Scherer and Bevans, *New Directions*, 36–88.
30. Bevans and Schroeder, *Constants*, 263.
31. Bosch, *Transforming Mission*, 482.
32. Scherer, *Gospel*, 163.
33. Newbigin, *Gospel*, 1.
34. Yates, *Christian Mission*, 243.

evangelical and progressive/minjung theology. Particularly minjung theology emerged out of Koreans' unique sociopolitical struggles for justice during the 1970s and 1980s as Park Joon-Sik aptly describes:

> Minjung theology affirms Korean culture and history as the context for a proper Korean theology, regarding the biblical stories and the social biographies of the suffering minjung (the mass of the people) as the two primary reference points . . . it has challenged Korean Christianity to be more integral and prophetic in its theology and practice of mission and to be on the side of the marginalized minjung.[35]

Minjung theology, however, was popular mostly among educated intellectuals, theologians, and academics. This remains an irony because the minjung themselves were often not the actual agents in developing and promoting a theology for ordinary Koreans. Most Korean Christians instead sided with the orthodox, evangelical camp, which underscored individual salvation and change. The evangelical Korean Christians thus paid less attention to the importance of Christian social action compared to their progressive counterparts. Korean Christian humanitarian mission, that is concerned with social justice and philanthropy, emerged in the late 1980s and the early 1990s. It did so as the Korean economy developed and as Korea became increasingly democratized following the election of the first civilian President in 1992. Also, the global political milieu drastically shifted in the aftermath of the collapse of communism beginning in 1989 and this called for global humanitarianism to assist the former communist nations. The rapid mushrooming of Korean Christian humanitarian mission NGOs is remarkable, especially considering the fact that the history of Korean global mission began in the late 1970s. Thus the range of theology of mission in Korea has been expanded since the rise of its humanitarian mission. In other words, Christian mission in Korea now not only entails the evangelical, ecclesial, and moral task, but also the humanitarian task that includes serving the poor and tackling global injustices.

Here I would like to briefly examine the mission theology of three Korean Christian organizations to show the diversifying mission theology of Korean Christianity: (a) the evangelical mission theology of Korean Presbyterian Global Mission Society (GMS), (b) the holistic evangelical mission theology of KFHI, (c) and the humanitarian mission theology

---

35. Park, "Korean Protestant," 61.

of GN. First of all, Korean Presbyterian Global Mission Society understands mission as spreading the gospel and evangelizing the world. This strictly evangelistic interpretation of mission derives its scriptural basis from Matt 28:18-20, which leads to the missionary mandate of world evangelization. It appears true that this type of evangelistically motivated mission is still the most widely accepted and common way to do mission work for most Korean Christians. With this strong evangelistic motive, GMS focuses on building churches around the globe, training pastors, and sharing the gospel with locals. They would not necessarily reject the importance of humanitarian mission, but their fundamental goal is to spread the gospel. While there are overlaps such as the evangelistic motive, KFHI values both evangelism and social action. In doing this, they heavily rely on two parts of the Scripture, Matt 28:18-20 and Luke 4:18-19 in which both evangelism (spiritual) and humanitarian care (physical) are emphasized. KFHI's humanitarian operations use the global Korean Christian network that has mostly been organized and strengthened by Christian church communities, mainly through Korean immigrants. Although KFHI understands that many Korean Christian donors want to see the instant growth of Christianity in developing countries, they also make it clear that both physical and spiritual dimensions of human development should go hand in hand. In contrast to the previous two organizations, GN's mission theology resonates with its interest in improving the quality of human life inspired by Christian faith based on Luke 4:18-19 and James 2:15-17 within which Christian charity and action are underscored. GN, thus, implements its humanitarian projects primarily in cooperation with the Korean government and business corporations. GN does not necessarily hide its Christian origin; rather, it highlights the inspiration of Christian faith, which motivates their humanitarian work that accepts everyone regardless of his/her background. With this historical development of mission theology in Korea in mind, now I would like to examine the mission theology—particularly in relation to public mission theology—and practical theology of Korean Christian humanitarian NGOs. My use of the term "public mission theology" refers specifically to mission theology that shows interests in the common or public good, which surpasses cultural, sociopolitical, and religious boundaries. Also, I use the term "practical theology" in order to examine practices of the Korean Christian humanitarian NGOs that potentially lead to theological, critical reflection—for example, intercultural and interfaith dimensions.

# 4

## Theology of Mission and Practical Theology

CHRISTIAN HUMANITARIAN NGOS NEED to be rooted in sound theology in order to undertake their mission in a coherent and consistent manner. In this chapter, I focus on the mission theology of the two organizations—KFHI and GN—from which their mission practices originate. I do so in conjunction with some of the broader discourses in theology of mission and practical theology. First, I examine the diversifying public mission theology of Korean Christian humanitarian NGOs. Then the second section discusses the influence of holistic evangelical, mainline Protestant, and Catholic theologies of mission on Korean Christian humanitarian NGOs. I close the chapter by exploring questions concerning intercultural and interfaith dimensions of Korean Christian humanitarian NGOs.

### THE DIVERSIFYING PUBLIC MISSION THEOLOGY OF KOREAN CHRISTIAN HUMANITARIAN NGOS

Many Korean Christians want to engage in public interests and in this process diverse public mission theologies emerge and impact their actual practices as KFHI and GN illustrate, whether it is KFHI's ecclesial mission theology or GN's humanitarian mission theology. Before examining KFHI's and GN's mission theologies that are pertinent to public theology, I want to discuss some of the major discourses in public theology. The growing popularity of the term public theology seems to derive from various motivating factors. The very nature of our globalizing world, which has raised people's awareness of global challenges including global epidemics, poverty, economic disparity, and human rights, demands the development of Christian theology that could engage in such publicly critical matters.[1] Also, many contemporary Christians seek to make their Christian faith relevant to the secular society in a reciprocal manner.[2] In other words, they want to see active interactions between God's word and its manifestations (or God's works) in and through our globalizing world. By promoting public theology, these Christians cultivate the "prophetic vocation of missional congregations as public companions,"[3] thus challenging the ecclesial boundary of Christian faith and mission.[4] Finally, the work of Jürgen Habermas, an esteemed German philosopher and sociologist, who explored the importance of critical communicative theory has provided ample theoretical tools for public theology. Habermas argues that in order to form public opinion in our social life we need a public sphere as a common platform in which members of the society can enjoy rational, communicative conversations.[5] One of the most prominent areas for the communicative conversation relates to the communal, common good. Habermas' work on the public sphere has appealed to many Christian scholars who affirm the public nature of Christian faith and theology by putting emphasis on the public or common good.[6]

What then does public theology mean? Dirkie Smit discusses several definitions of public theology, notably "a narrower and general use of the term."[7] For the former, public theology is understood as a normative concept, which was developed alongside Western democratic culture, and it deliberately forms public opinion geared toward the common good. There are at least two extremes within this view. At one end of the spectrum, public theology is synonymous with a civil religion separated from particular church traditions. At the other end of the spectrum, public theology is considered as the divine calling of the church, which motivates people to promote the public good such as human dignity and human rights. The latter uses the term public theology in a general sense. In other words, the gospel, from its inception, has called believers to be public witnesses especially concerning the care of the weak and the mar-

---

1. Atherton, *Public Theology*, 2.
2. Forrester, *Christian Justice*, 31.
3. See Simpson, "Missional Congregations" and "Civil Society."
4. Chung, *Public Theology*, 2–3.
5. See Habermas, *Theory of Communication*.
6. Stackhouse, *Public Theology*, 20–21.
7. Hansen, *Christian in Public*, 11–46.

ginalized. Smit argues that there are also two extremes for this approach. At one end of the spectrum, public theology is interested in locating a specific public audience in light of David Tracy's three publics—the church, the academy, and society.[8] At the opposite end, public theology is exclusively oriented to and serves the public society as the only audience. In sum, there is no uniform definition or meaning of the term public theology. Rather, due to the complexity of one's view on "public" in conjunction with one's context, public theology comes in many different forms.[9] Whatever forms it takes, however, public theology appears to include the following characteristics: (1) it is interested in the social, external spheres of human experience; (2) it is not confined to the ecclesial sphere; (3) it mobilizes faith communities to promote global issues such as justice, peace, and human rights; and (4) it tends to foster partnerships with other religious traditions.[10]

The above definition and characteristics of public theology resonate deeply with a kind of theology that KFHI and GN want to promote. First of all, both NGOs lay great emphasis on the public, common good along with personal salvation and transformation. In other words, their mission is grounded in public theology that contributes to external dimensions of human life including community health, education, and human rights. This public theology thus legitimizes KFHI and GN's involvement in development. Second, KFHI and GN both mobilize faith communities to counteract global problems. However, they are not exclusively confined within the ecclesial boundary. Although KFHI encourages collaboration with churches around the world, it does not endorse a particular Christian denomination. GN, on the other hand, does not encourage any exclusive partnership with a particular religious tradition. Also, both NGOs value partnering with governments and business corporations. Finally, KFHI and GN work with people from different religious traditions other than Christianity. They both engage in interfaith partnership for different reasons. KFHI is more likely to see it as an opportunity to share the gospel with unbelievers whereas GN tends to understand it as a way to show the love of Christ. I delve into this interfaith dimension later in the chapter. In sum, both KFHI and GN have and promote a type

---

8. See Tracy, *Analogical Imagination*.
9. Hansen, *Christian in Public*, 42–43.
10. Chung, *Public Theology*, 3.

of public theology, which is differentiated from private, denominational, and sectarian theology.

In terms of the historical development of public theology, Paul Chung in his *Public Theology in an Age of World Christianity* lays out three noticeable attempts to formulate public theology.[11] First of all, there are individuals who highlight the public role that institutional, ecclesial communities should play.[12] Influenced by Clifford Geertz's concept of "thick description,"[13] which underlines a detailed, descriptive understanding of socio-cultural and moral contexts, these individuals attempt to provide a Christian belief in accord with Christian faith and ecclesial traditions. Secondly, there are scholars who attempt to connect the public realm of theological discourse inter-disciplinarily with social sciences.[14] For example, David Tracy, in light of Habermas' theory of communicative action, constructs a complex, interdisciplinary model—the revised correlation method—within which public theology entails fundamental, hermeneutical, systematical, and practical dimensions.[15] Finally, the third proposal fosters theological discourse that promotes the common good for all humanity, thus "transcending the boundaries between religious and secular spheres."[16]

While both KFHI and GN promote a type of public theology, they exemplify two different public theologies that directly and indirectly affect their humanitarian operations. On the one hand, KFHI's ecclesial public theology appears to be rooted in its strong emphasis on both physical and spiritual dimensions of human development. God is understood as a holistic being who sends us not only to share the good news of Jesus Christ but also to meet physical needs. Within this theology, KFHI's collaboration with local churches along with other political, educational, and socio-cultural organizations can be justified. This ecclesial public theology then resonates somewhat with Chung's first group, which engages in public theology with Christian faith and church traditions in mind. On the other hand, GN's humanitarian public theology seems to focus strongly on Christian practice of love and justice rather than

---

11. Ibid., 4.
12. See Marty, *Public Church*, and Thiemann, *Constructing*.
13. Geertz, *Interpretation*, 10.
14. See Tracy, *Analogical Imagination*, and Stackhouse, *Public Theology*.
15. See Tracy, *Blessed Rage*.
16. Valentine, *Mapping*, 87.

evangelization. That is, they believe that Christian's faith-inspired acts of love and justice to improve the quality of human life can potentially lead to witnessing Christian faith to others without enforcing it. In this, GN's public theology reflects Chung's third group, which views the goal of public theology as actualizing the common good for all humanity crossing multiple boundaries. Within this theology, GN intentionally clarifies that it does not exclusively work with Christian churches around the world. Thus, its projects are undertaken in partnership with a variety of agents such as the local government, schools, hospitals, civil society groups, along with religious communities. This leads to an important question: In what ways then has the wider discourse in theology of mission impacted the above public theological development of Korean Christian humanitarian NGOs?

## THE INFLUENCE OF HOLISTIC EVANGELICAL, MAINLINE PROTESTANT, AND CATHOLIC THEOLOGIES OF MISSION ON KOREAN CHRISTIAN HUMANITARIAN NGOS

Two prominent Catholic theologians, Stephen Bevans and Roger Schroeder, in light of theological paradigms developed by Justo Gonzalez and Dorothee Solle, chart three distinctive theologies of mission: Type A (mission as saving souls and extending the Church), Type B (mission as discovery of the truth), and Type C (mission as commitment to liberation and transformation).[17] The three types of theologies of mission are categorized based on various factors: Christology, Ecclesiology, Eschatology, Salvation, Anthropology, and Culture. Type A theology generally represents basic theological grounds in which many evangelical Christians stand, while Type B and Type C theologies denote the overall theological directions of both Catholic and Mainline Protestant traditions.[18] In this section, I first examine three different mission theologies that have influenced theologies of evangelical, ecumenical (mainline Protestant), and Catholic Christians.[19] Then I locate mission theologies of Korean Christian humanitarian NGOs in light of the three theological frameworks of mission.

---

17. See Solle, *Thinking*, and Gonzalez, *Christian Thought*.

18. Bevans and Schroeder, *Constants*, 352.

19. I believe Christology, Ecclesiology, and Eschatology of the three distinctive theologies of mission lend important theological implications to the Korean Christian Humanitarian NGOs.

*Type A Theology and Evangelicals: Mission as Saving Souls and Extending the Church.*

A) Christology

Type A theology understands Jesus Christ in line with the orthodox, doctrinal portrayal of his reality, "one divine person who possessed two distinct natures, human and divine,"[20] and it tends to downplay the meaning of the historical Jesus. Type A theology endorses an exclusive Christology that "confesses Jesus alone as Savior and without explicit faith in Christ one has no hope of salvation."[21] Influenced by this exclusive Christology, countless missionaries in the eighteenth and nineteenth centuries such as William Carey devoted their lives to save souls and plant churches. Later in the late nineteenth century, many evangelicals adopted the Type A Christology. For example, in 1974 the Lausanne Covenant specified that "there is only one Savior and one gospel (Gal 1:6–9)"[22] and in 1989 the *Manila Manifesto* reaffirmed that "other religions and ideologies are not alternative paths to God . . . Christ is the only way."[23]

B) Ecclesiology

Type A theology's understanding of mission is essentially ecclesial, regarding the church as "the sole agent and protector of faith in Christ."[24] In exploring theology that concerns the nature and mission of the church, Avery Dulles, a renowned American Catholic theologian of the post-Vatican II era, provides a useful framework that includes five different models of the church: institution, mystical communion, sacrament, herald, and servant.[25] Within this framework, the church-centered ecclesiology of the Catholic Church, with its upholding of the church's visible structure, represents Dulles's institutional model. Also, many evangelical churches that put emphasis on the structural hierarchy (e.g., the senior pastor's charismatic, authoritative role) and the importance of proclamation and

---

20. Jenkins, *Next Christendom*, 51.
21. Bevans and Schroeder, *Constants*, 40.
22. Scherer and Bevans, *New Directions*, 254.
23. Ibid., 293.
24. Bevans and Schroeder, *Constants*, 40.
25. See Avery Dulles, *Models*.

preaching in and through the church belong to the institutional model.[26] Type A ecclesiology is inclined to understand the fundamental objective of missionary activity as the extension of the church, thus constructing visible ecclesial structures around the world. Therefore, Christian mission, according to Type A ecclesiology, can only be justified within the boundary of the church, especially the formal and visible establishment of the church.

c) *Eschatology*

Alister McGrath, a British theologian at Kings College London, lays out three distinct theological perspectives on the end of time or eschatology: futurist eschatology (the end time is to come in the future), realized eschatology (the end time is already realized in a personal, internal manner), and inaugurated eschatology (the end time is already inaugurated but not yet fully accomplished).[27] Type A eschatology generally supports the belief that the end of time will entail God's judgment of the world in which the good will be lifted up to heaven and the evil will be eternally condemned in hell. In other words, God's judgment could take place at any time in the future; thus it is considered futurist eschatology. Because of its apocalyptic inclination, Type A eschatology tends to disregard the role of the world and human history in the scheme of salvation; rather it focuses on the importance of "keeping the divine commands" in order to be saved.[28] This type of eschatology has inspired mission of many theologically conservative Christians who felt the imminence of Christ's second coming. One example comes from those who believed in dispensationalism, which divides the history of salvation into several unique periods based on 1 Thess 4:15–17 including rapture and the coming of Christ as Christians are "caught up in the air."[29] Alerted by the dispensational eschatology, many evangelical Christians devoted their entire lives to proclaiming the gospel in order to save people from the final judgment in hell.

One of the most important concepts that deserves particular attention as regards evangelicals' eschatology is millennium or a thousand-year rule of Jesus Christ. Many evangelical Christians have been interested

26. Solle, *Thinking*, 148.
27. McGrath, *Christian Theology*, 470.
28. Bevans and Schroeder, *Constants*, 43.
29. McGrath, *Christian Theology*, 472.

in developing a doctrine of eschatology related to the concept of millennium based on the book of Revelation chapter twenty. With distinct hermeneutical principles, those Christians have argued over such ideas as the time of "a millennial Kingdom" and "the parousia—the second coming of Christ," resulting in three major eschatological constructs: postmillennialism, amillennialism, and premillennialism.[30] Historically speaking, amillennialism was the most long-lasting eschatological position beginning from the time of St. Augustine in the fourth century to the seventeenth century popularized by the Puritans. Then postmillennialism, with an emphasis on both proclamation of the gospel and social action, becomes the most dominant eschatological position during the succeeding two centuries until the late nineteenth century. Premillennialism, first upheld by pre-Augustinian church fathers, resurfaced in the late nineteenth century and has become increasingly popular among fundamentalists and conservative evangelicals. I highlight the theme of millennialism in this section because, as it will become clear, one's eschatological positioning has greatly influenced his/her involvement in society and culture including challenging injustice, improving human conditions, and promoting education. This thus directly relates to the humanitarian aspect of Christian mission.

1) *Postmillennialism*

Postmillennialism takes a figurative approach in interpreting Revelation 20, positing the idea of millennium within the scheme of human history that precedes the second coming of Christ. The postmillennial understanding is well articulated in the following:

> Those who hold the postmillennial view believe that the Kingdom of God is now being extended in the world through the preaching of the gospel and the saving work of the Holy Spirit, that the world eventually is to be Christianized, and that the return of Christ will occur at the close of a long period of righteousness and peace, commonly called the millennium.[31]

Those who endorse the postmillennial eschatology understand the kingdom as something that is actualized not in a sudden, cataclysmic manner. Rather, they, in light of Jesus' parables of the mustard seed and the yeast (Matt 13:31–33), interpret the kingdom as a reality that will take

30. Samuel and Sugden, *Mission*, 137.
31. Boettner, *Millennium*, 4.

place gradually and call for Christians' participation in human history. This postmillennial view was widely accepted by evangelical Christians during the eighteenth and nineteenth centuries, spurred by the Great Awakening (1720–1740) coupled with the Puritan and Pietistic religious practices that aspired to complete the Great Commission as indicated in Matt 28:18–20.[32] Some of the most outstanding figures who held this position include John and Charles Wesley, Jonathan Edwards, and Charles Hodge, and they demonstrated a strong social concern both on individual and structural levels.[33] For example, Christians such as William Wilberforce and John Newton fought against the evil of slavery and showed concern for the poor.[34] Since postmillennialism believes in "the gradual improvement and redemption of the world," it tends to be optimistic about the course of human history, which will be culminated in "a golden age of prosperity, justice, and peace."[35] Because of this optimistic outlook, those who support the postmillennial view underscore Christian social activism by advocating human rights, feeding the hungry, and improving health and education.

2) *Amillennialism*

Also known as non-millennialism, amillennialism interprets Revelation chapter twenty in a "non-literal, non-temporal" way, thus understanding the millennium reign of God in "spiritual, non-earthly, and non-political" terms.[36] The amillennial view on the end times is summarized in the following phrase:

> The amillennial view is not a narrative account of a future earthly reign of peace at all. But it has the apocalyptic unveiling of the reality of salvation in Christ as a backdrop to the reality of the suffering and martyrdom that still continue as long as the dominion of Christ remains hidden.[37]

Amillennialism was the popular eschatology for more than one thousand years, from the time of St. Augustine until the seventeenth century,[38] and

32. Marsden, *Fundamentalism*, 49.
33. See Smith, *Revivalism*.
34. Bosch, *Witness*, 147.
35. Samuel and Sugden, *Mission*, 138.
36. Ibid., 139.
37. Berkouwer, *Return*, 307.
38. Armerding and Gasque, *Handbook of Biblical Prophecy*, 43.

it was largely accepted by the Protestant Reformers.[39] Amillennialism, in spite of sharing an affinity with the premillennialism's pessimistic outlook on the conditions of the world and culture, tends not to be interested in "signs of the times."[40] Those who take the amillennial approach disagree with postmillennialists' strong belief in a golden age of peace and justice—an ideal kingdom on earth as a result of spreading the gospel to the entire world.

### 3) PREMILLENNIALISM

Premillennialism is based upon the belief that the second coming of Christ will precede a millennium, and this approach is the most common and popular eschatological view of our times among conservative evangelicals.[41] It puts a great emphasis on the power of evil in the world, which will be subdued by the apocalyptic, cataclysmic in-breaking of the reign of Jesus Christ who brings forth peace, justice, and prosperity. The rise of premillennial eschatology began with the Civil War in America and reached its climax in the aftermath of the two world wars as the pessimism about the progress of humanity increased. Dispensationalism, as a form of premillennial eschatology that acknowledges God's apocalyptic intervention in human history through several chronological periods, is a recently popularized concept in America through countless revivals, conferences, and publications, further influencing fundamentalist Christians.[42] When it comes to Christian mission, premillennialism reversed the postmillennial holistic understanding of mission (preaching of the gospel alongside Christian's involvement in political action and social reform) by emphasizing the hopeless nature of human efforts for progress and an abandonment of the sinful world. As a result, American Evangelicalism began to lose its previous zeal for social action and responsibility.[43] Instead, those who were affected by the premillennial view started to withdraw from the worldly affairs and to focus solely on world evangelization so that they can save as many souls as possible prior to the return of Christ.[44] In doing this, Jesus' remark in Matt 24:14, which alludes to

39. See Quistorp, *Calvin's Doctrine*.
40. Erickson, *Contemporary*, 75.
41. Samuel and Sugden, *Mission*, 141.
42. See Bass, *Backgrounds*.
43. Weber, *Living*, 183.
44. Dayton, *Discovering*, 127.

the correlation between the preaching of the gospel to all nations and the end of the world, becomes premillennialists' quintessential scriptural basis. Nevertheless, it is important to note that premillennialism played a key role in a variety of mission mobilizations at the dawn of the twentieth century through "the Student Volunteer Movement, faith missions, and missionary training schools and Bible institutes," which sent thousands of missionaries overseas.[45] This leads to the possibility that Christians in the non-Western world, who interacted with the Western missionaries during the twentieth century, might have been impacted by the Western missionaries' premillennial eschatology.

## Type B Theology and Ecumenicals / Catholics: Mission as Discovery of the Truth

A) CHRISTOLOGY

Type B Christology, similar to Type A, initially underscored the divinity of Jesus Christ—a high Christology, although unlike the orthodox approach of Type A it encouraged debates and generated disputes.[46] However, upon the dawn of modernity, human reason became the focus of Type B theology and its Christology began to highlight the Jesus of history—a low Christology. Tracing its theological roots back to Origen, the first Christian systematic theologian, Type B Christology understands the role of Jesus Christ in salvation as revelatory,[47] making God's love visible to humanity. Thus, Type B Christology negates Type A's understanding of redemption—satisfying the punitive God, replacing it with the revelatory, redemptive work of Jesus Christ who draws Christians to the truth of God's love. Type B Christology later became influential among Catholics and liberal Protestant theologians in North America, especially during the nineteenth and the early twentieth century, who supported an inclusive approach to other religions and salvation.[48] However, Type B Christology considers missionary activity vital not in the sense that we need to save those who have not heard the gospel from

---

45. Weber, *Living*, 73–81.
46. Gonzalez, *Christian Thought*, 84.
47. Walls, "Old Athens," 149.
48. Bevans and Schroeder, *Constants*, 53.

eternal damnation, but because "all peoples can reach their full potential in Christ and profit from the full understanding of Christ."[49]

B) *ECCLESIOLOGY*

Type B's ecclesiology is deeply related to its Christology that underlines revelation and illumination. In other words, as people who are illuminated and experience the revelatory love of God through Christ, Christians cultivate a community of faith within which they continue to encourage one another and witness to all peoples around the world. In this, Type B ecclesiology reflects what the French priest and philosopher Teilhard de Chardin portrayed the church as "reflexively Christified portion of the world,"[50] demonstrating a model community for all humankind. Type B ecclesiology, in reference to Avery Dulles's framework, elicits characteristics similar to the mystical communion model or sacrament model. Specifically, the Type B ecclesiology is based upon reaching the intimate connection to Christ through illumination and it emphasizes the church's role as an instrument to bring about the unity of all humanity with God and with one another.[51] One noteworthy aspect, concerning Type B ecclesiology, is that the church, while representing Christ's presence in the world, is not necessarily confined to its outward, visible construction as in Type A ecclesiology. In the late twentieth century, many Protestant mainline denominations (ecumenicals) and the Catholic Church adopted the Type B ecclesiology. For example, it is aptly captured in the Vatican Council II's decree on the church, which describes the church as "a people brought into unity from the unity of the Father, the Son, and the Holy Spirit."[52] When it comes to the motive for missionary activity, Type B ecclesiology advocates the belief that the church needs to reach out to the world to witness its illuminating, revelatory experiences to others and promote unity.

C) *ESCHATOLOGY*

Based upon Type B theology's strong optimism about human lives and history, Type B eschatology fosters a sense of hopefulness about the present

---

49. Walls, *Missionary*, introduction 17.
50. Gutierrez, *Theology*, 261.
51. Bevans and Schroeder, *Constants*, 55.
52. Ibid., 55.

reality of humanity, thus it is characterized as "realized eschatology."[53] This optimistic inclination of Type B theology derives from Origen's theory of restoration in which "God is calling all intellectual creatures (even the devil) back to the original unity" for the eschatological reestablishement.[54] Type B eschatology alongside Origen's optimism later influenced modern liberal theology. For example, Adolf Harnack alluded to the view that the end of time is something already available to believers now by saying: "The kingdom of God comes by coming to the individual, by entering into his soul and laying hold of it . . . it is not a question of angels and devils, thrones and principalities, but of God and the soul, the soul and its God."[55] Also, Paul Tillich demonstrated this type of realized eschatology by highlighting the role of Jesus as "New Being" who joins humanity with "full eschatological power" when we experience faith in our individual historical context.[56] Since Type B eschatology understands the end of history or the reign of God as something that is already realized through Jesus Christ and exists amongst us, the task of mission becomes inviting people to reach their maximum potential through faith in Jesus Christ geared toward fullness of life.

## Type C Theology and Ecumenicals / Catholics: Mission as Transforming Liberation

A) CHRISTOLOGY

Type C theology finds its origin in Irenaeus who was deeply pastoral in his approach to theology believing that "God is involved in history and is manifest in radically historical ways."[57] He proclaimed that "Jesus Christ and the Holy Spirit are two hands of God" alluding to his strong affirmation of God's engagement in the world's history.[58] In accord with the theology of Irenaeus, Type C Christology is based on Jesus Christ's liberating role in human history as the incarnation of God's love, which has been present with us since the beginning. When it comes to the issue of

---

53. McGrath, *Christian*, 470.
54. Bevans and Schroeder, *Constants*, 56–57.
55. Harnack, *What is Christianity?*, 51.
56. Tillich, *Systematic Theology*, 118–38.
57. Bevans and Schroeder, *Constants*, 63.
58. Ibid., 63.

redemption, Type C Christology does not relate Christ's redeeming work to atonement or the offering of a noble illumination as found in the two previous theologies. Rather, it understands Jesus' redemptive work as the accomplishment of our liberation in that Jesus, through his life, death, and resurrection, freed us from our oppression.[59] The Type C Christology, especially its understanding of redemption as liberation, made a huge impact on a variety of liberation theologies that have sprung up since the 1970s. In its approach to other religions, Type C Christology tends to take a moderately pluralist position due to its practical interest in human liberation. In a similar vein, Type C Christology does not underscore the proclamation of a message or propagating of doctrines, but it highlights the saving power of Jesus Christ through our life of liberating witness.[60]

B) *Ecclesiology*

The key word for Type C's ecclesiology is history in the sense that it stresses the important role of the church in human history. In other words, the church, as the embodiment of Christ, has the obligation to play a herald or servant role, raising historical consciousness and addressing human concerns such as liberating the oppressed. Type C's ecclesial commitment to history became more visible in the late twentieth century among Catholics and ecumenical Protestants. For example, Catholic ecclesiology experienced an immense shift following the Second Vatican Council, which affirmed the church's role in human history, especially concerning the marginalized. Type C ecclesiology was also exemplified by a prominent liberation theologian Gustavo Gutierrez, who identified the church with the "sacrament of liberation."[61] Gutierrez thus put emphasis on God's liberating work in human history through the church and its witnesses in life and action. Furthermore, a Brazilian theologian Leonardo Boff used the phrase "reinventing the church" in explaining the importance of the local community (the base ecclesial community) in which local leaders become the active agents geared toward actualizing a church "not just for the poor but of the poor."[62]

---

59. Ibid., 64.
60. Ibid., 65.
61. Ibid., 66.
62. See Boff, *Ecclesiogenesis*.

c) ESCHATOLOGY

Type C's eschatology, in light of Type C theology's overall emphasis on historical reality, does not understand eschatology as something that entails a dramatic inauguration of "a timeless, spiritual state."[63] Rather, influenced by Irenaeus's theology, Type C eschatology upholds the idea that the present history encounters cosmic transformation upon the final consummation.[64] Teilhard de Chardin underscored that the church is commissioned to the world in preparation for our ultimate consummation of wholeness in Jesus Christ.[65] Type C eschatology, therefore, can be described as "inaugurated eschatology"[66] in the sense that the reign of God was inaugurated by Jesus Christ but it has not been fulfilled yet through the final consummation. The task of mission in Type C eschatology then relates to God's salvific action breaking into the present human history in various forms such as political freedom and human rights.

Throughout the history of Christianity, the aforementioned three mission theologies seem to have shaped contours of Christian mission, influencing various Christian denominations. More importantly, their mission theologies have often converged and diverged. One of the most recent examples comes from the study of Rodger Bassham, a well-known mission scholar, who explores the development of three major mission theologies—evangelical, ecumenical, and Roman Catholic—from 1948 to 1975. To understand major characteristics of the three aforementioned theologies of mission, Bassham examines their theological similarities and differences by investigating both convergence and divergence.[67] Bassham admits that there have been continuous efforts to find consensus within the three streams—evangelical, conciliar Protestant, and Roman Catholic—over the past few decades. For example, all three agree on key theological issues such as their shift from a church-centric understanding of mission to a trinitarian one geared toward the Missio Dei and the need for unity in mission and engagement with other religious traditions.[68] However, certain distinctions are still clearly made in spite of the emerging convergence in mission theology. For instance, each stream envisions

---

63. Bevans and Schroeder, *Constants*, 63.
64. Gonzalez, *Christian Thought*, 133.
65. See Teilhard de Chardin, *Phenomenon of Man*.
66. McGrath, *Christian Theology*, 470.
67. Bassham, *Mission Theology*, 358.
68. Ibid., 331.

different ideals and goals regarding unity in mission (e.g., structural, organic, spiritual unity) and engaging with other religious traditions (e.g., the ultimate purpose of doing this: evangelization, acknowledging other faith traditions as spiritual equals, promoting peace).

When it comes to Korean Christian humanitarian NGOs, the holistic-evangelical (with more emphasis on evangelism)[69] and the mainline Protestant, Catholic (with more emphasis on faith-inspired humanitarian action) theologies of mission have been influential. For example, the holistic-evangelical mission theology is clearly stated and practiced in KFHI's humanitarian work, which equally highlights spiritual and physical dimensions of human development. This type of holistic mission theology—promoting multiple dimensions of human needs—that derives from the evangelical tradition represents the majority of Christian humanitarian NGOs in Korea. In examining KFHI's theology of mission, I draw upon my participatory observations and interviews with KFHI missionaries (field staff and volunteers) in Kumi, Uganda, which I undertook during the summer of 2008 and the fall of 2011. There are currently about twenty Korean missionaries who are involved in KFHI's aid and development programs (e.g., medical mission, teaching, health and sanitation, water development, local church support, children's program, microfinance, etc.) in a rural town called Kumi located in the northeastern part of Uganda. By working as a visiting professor and chaplain during the fall semester in 2011 at Kumi University (KFHI's major education program), I had numerous opportunities to interview the Korean missionaries concerning their theological grounding of mission in the midst of development practices.

First of all, KFHI tends to exemplify Type A's exclusive Christology, which understands Jesus Christ as the divine, sole Savior of our sins and the only path to salvation. For example, in response to my question "Who is Jesus Christ to you or what is your understanding of Jesus Christ?," most KFHI field workers in Kumi included the following statement: "Jesus Christ sacrificed himself to wash away our sins and we can only be saved by the blood of Christ."

Secondly, KFHI strongly supports the ecclesiology demonstrated in Type A theology, which underscores the extension of the visible ecclesial structures around the world and regards the church as the guardian of faith in Christ. This is shown among many KFHI staff members in Kumi

---

69. I use the term "holistic-evangelical" in order to designate some evangelicals who believe in the importance of both evangelism and social action.

who prefer to work with local Christian congregations as opposed to government officials and business entrepreneurs. Specifically, they not only provide financial assistance to the local Christians who intend to construct a church building but also collaborate with local churches while undertaking a variety of development programs. For example, I was able to observe KFHI's ecclesial development approach while shadowing its recent rural economic development project through tilapia fish-farming in Kumi. As soon as KFHI staff with expertise in fish-farming found a suitable location for the project, they contacted a nearby local Christian congregation. They then set up a community meeting at the church to train local church leaders by giving them information and instructions concerning how to install essential equipment such as nets and poles, maintain the facilities, and to sell the fish for profits. One salient factor in this process is that KFHI field officers partnered exclusively with local congregation leaders from this church nearby the lake. They did so with the hope that the local Christians will eventually take over the entire management of this community income-generating program. This ecclesial inclination of KFHI missionaries in Kumi can also be found in their own Christian practices. For example, it is common for them to attend more than two different worship services (usually one with local Ugandans and the other with Korean expatriates) on Sundays. In doing so, they emphasize the importance of keeping the Sabbath holy within the ecclesial boundaries. In sum, KFHI illustrates the strong acknowledgement of the church as the fundamental base of missionary activities.

Finally, concerning eschatology, KFHI somewhat resonates with Type A eschatology. I asked the following question to several KFHI missionaries in Kumi: "What are your thoughts on the kingdom of God and the end of time in light of your mission work?" The most common answer was related to Type A's futurist eschatology:

> I believe that the end of time comes with some kind of final judgment of God, like some going to heaven and others going to hell. And the kingdom of God will take place sometime in the future. So I think it is very important to share the gospel with the unbelievers before it is too late . . . but I also think that our inviting of people to Christ has to accompany meeting their physical needs. You cannot simply talk about something spiritual to someone who is hungry, naked, or homeless.

This answer, on the one hand, reflects Type A eschatology's emphasis on proclaiming the gospel to save people from the final judgment. On the other hand, unlike the ignoring of the world represented in Type A eschatology, KFHI missionaries want to be involved in human history by challenging critical global issues.

Earlier in this chapter, I explained the three streams of eschatological thoughts in conjunction with the concept of millennium, which have historically been developed and contested among evangelical Christians. Considering the fact that KFHI introduces itself as a "holistic evangelical" mission organization to the public, it poses an inquiry about KFHI missionaries' understanding of "the millennium." As I previously described, one of the most distinctive differences between postmillennialists and premillennialists has to do with their view of the world—either redemptive or hopeless—and it has affected the ways in which they understand and undertake missionary work. Although KFHI missionaries are generally less interested in doctrinal arguments concerning the millennium, they, somewhat similar to the premillennialist view, tend to view the world as a sinful place. However, instead of abandoning or escaping from the world, they want to be involved in secular affairs, counteracting injustices and improving human conditions of the world. This postmillennial inclination is epitomized in the following excerpts from my interview with KFHI's Dr. Chung:

> The Scripture tells us that God is the only one who knows the time and place for the end of the world and we should not be entangled in some kind of serious debate concerning the end of the world. It also says that we have to bring out the gospel to the entire world. Having said that, I believe the return of Christ will take place as the world evangelization is completed. In awaiting the second coming of Christ, however, we Christians need to proclaim the gospel to the world both through word and social action. They are two sides of the coin that cannot be separated from one another.

This eschatological grounding exemplifies that KFHI wants to demonstrate the love of Jesus Christ and witness to the world, ultimately geared toward accomplishing the Great Commission in Matt 28:18–20.

Differentiated from KFHI, it is interesting that GN does not specifically state its Christian identity either on its mission statement or on its public website overall. GN's subtle theology of mission perhaps demonstrates an emerging way to do public theology of mission that could minimize potential conflicts with the secular society and maximize its legitimacy to be an impartial partner in taking on global concerns. In this,

## Theology of Mission and Practical Theology 69

GN's theology of mission has an affinity with mainline Protestant and Roman Catholic theologies of mission, which are traditionally inclined to faith-inspired, humanitarian action. In examining GN's theology of mission, I use my interviews with its CEO, Rev. Lee Il-Ha, along with GN's public documents available online.[70] First of all, GN's Christology reflects Type B's focus on Jesus Christ's revelatory illumination of God's love for humanity and Type C's emphasis on Christ's liberating role in human history as the incarnation of God's love. GN's CEO, Lee Il-Ha says:

> I understand Jesus Christ as the ultimate demonstration of God's love for us. We not only accept the love of God but also have to share it with our neighbors around the world through our actions. In other words, I am assured that we have a divine obligation to liberate the marginalized from poverty and injustice.

GN's Christology, which is centered upon the incarnate love of God through Jesus Christ, therefore, runs counter to KFHI's Christology that highlights the sacrificial atonement of Christ. Secondly, GN's ecclesiology is in accord with Type B ecclesiology: the church as an instrument for unity of humanity that reaches out to the world to witness the revelatory love of God demonstrated through Jesus Christ. Thus, the church is not necessarily being confined to its visible construction. Also, GN's ecclesiology appears to be aptly represented in Type C ecclesiology: its emphasis on the church's role as a prophetic servant that liberates the oppressed in order to embody the love of Christ. GN's CEO, Rev. *Lee* clarified this understanding in our interview:

> As you can see in our official website, we publicly announce that GN does not work exclusively with Christian churches . . . Yes, Christian churches have a key role to play in terms of doing global mission. I don't deny it. But I also think in order to embody the love of Christ, Christian mission needs to go beyond our church boundaries.

GN's ecclesiology, which pays great attention to mission in the secular world, is clearly different from KFHI's church-oriented development mission. Finally, GN's eschatology seems to reflect both Type B theology's "realized eschatology" and Type C theology's "inaugurated eschatology." For the former, since the kingdom of God has already been accomplished on earth, the task of mission is to help people reach their full potential in Christ. For the latter, since the reign of God was initiated by Christ

---

70. I interviewed Rev. Lee Il-Ha, in the summer of 2010 at his office in Seoul.

but has not been fulfilled yet, the task of mission is to bring forth God's liberatory transformation through our historical engagement waiting upon the final consummation. Rev. Lee, in our interview, answered my question "What is your eschatology?" in following ways:

> I believe that the kingdom of heaven is already at my heart but still yet to come. On the one hand, the kingdom of God has been actualized when Jesus Christ came to us, which means now we need to do our best to reach our full potential in our life. On the other hand, we, as Christians, look forward to God's ultimate transformation of the world at the end of time.

Thus, GN's eschatology, which focuses on the present reality hoping for the liberating and transforming future, differs from KFHI's eschatology in which the kingdom of God upon the final judgment is located sometime in the future.

## INTERCULTURAL AND INTERFAITH DIMENSIONS OF KOREAN CHRISTIAN HUMANITARIAN NGOS

This section discusses ways in which Korean Christian humanitarian NGOs deal with intercultural and interfaith issues. By doing so, I hope to support the following claims: Korean Christian humanitarian NGOs have the increasing desire to promote interculturalism and many Korean expatriates, despite cultural differences and challenges, strive to foster emotional solidarity in light of their own development experience. Furthermore, they have laid the groundwork for interreligious cooperation by working with communities of different faiths to varying degrees.

### *What are the intercultural dimensions of Korean Christian humanitarian NGOs?*

First, Korean NGO missionaries seem to adjust quickly to their host country's cultural environment. However, their adjustment to a new culture does not necessarily guarantee cultural sensitivity based on mutual respect and reciprocity. The high level of adaptability of many Korean NGO missionaries who work in a developing cultural context derives from some of the most distinctive Korean cultural elements such as Korean's valuing of harmony, perceptiveness, and relationship. Influenced by the Confucian value system, Korean culture has a tendency to encourage achieving harmony in the midst of building good relationships with others. For example, I had an opportunity to visit a group of Korean missionaries in Chiapas, Mexico in 2011. Centered around the *Ichthus* School, which was founded by Mr. Lee Young-Yong, twenty Koreans were living harmoniously together at a housing complex along with hundreds of Mexican and American teaching staff and students. Commissioned by various mission agencies including KFHI, the Korean missionaries were involved in different mission projects that range from teaching high school mathematics to managing a tilapia fish farm to promoting fair-trade coffee. During my interview, Lee mentioned that he and his missionary coworkers make a conscious effort to respect each other and live harmoniously with locals. Lee added that he does so after witnessing some Korean missionaries who were not respectful of and sensitive to local cultures. Lee's approach of respect and harmony seemed to resonate well with my observations and conversations with Mexican and American staff members. Korean missionaries thus need to be intentional about respecting their host country's culture in order to maximize their potential advantage in cultural adjustment.

Also, the Korean concept *nunchi*, which is the subtle ability to read others' *kibun* (one's mood or state of mind) without asking or being informed by others, epitomizes the importance of being perceptive in interpersonal relationship. Therefore, when Korean NGO missionaries move to a new, different cultural context, they are inclined to adapt themselves quickly to the host culture with the hope to cultivate harmony and foster genuine relationships with locals by using a heightened sense of *nunchi* to understand their surroundings.

To explore further this Korean's relative advantage in encountering cultures in developing countries' cultural contexts—perhaps in contrast to their Western missionary counterparts, I refer to two studies: Hall's and Nisbett's. First, cultural value orientation is the concept used by many scholars in intercultural communication who study the relationship between cultural values and communication behaviors, and one of the most well recognized examples of the cultural value orientation is Hall's Culture Context Model. Edward T. Hall divides cultural differences into two categories, low-context culture and high-context culture:

> In low-context communication, a direct verbal-expression style is the key: the situational context is not emphasized; self-expression, verbal fluency, and eloquent speech are valued; and people tend to directly express their opinions and intend to persuade others to accept their viewpoints. . . . In contrast,

in high-context communication, an indirect verbal-expression style is the key: explicit verbal messages are not emphasized; important information is usually carried in contextual cues such as place, time, situation, and relationship; harmony is highly valued; and people tend to talk around the point and avoid saying no directly to others.[71]

Hall's categorization of high-context culture, which comprises most non-Western countries including Korea, alludes to that Korean's high-context culture could become a great advantage in terms of interacting with people in other non-Western, developing cultural contexts. However, Hall's model poses many weaknesses to accept at face value. For example, Hall, by categorizing multiple countries into two different cultural groups, puts himself in a danger of being considered simplistic, ignoring the multifaceted nature of our rapidly globalizing cultures. Also, Hall undermines distinctive individual characteristics by overplaying simplified cultural features. In other words, as a counter-argument to Hall's theory, it is very plausible to encounter a quiet, perceptive, and introverted American alongside a vocal, expressive, and extroverted Korean. In sum, Hall's cultural value orientation model, despite its usefulness in terms of understanding two types of cultural communication, requires a great deal of further modification.

Richard Nisbett, who has taught psychology at Yale and University of Michigan, conducted research in order to find out why his graduate students from Korea, Japan, and China engage in their work differently from his American and European students. Nisbett observed that Asian students tend to formulate a contextual, holistic argument as opposed to linear logic, show a great deal of obedience to their advisors and seniors, feel comfortable with decisions made by the group instead of individualized choices.[72] One of Nisbett's findings has to do with the importance of relationship among Asians.[73] Asians tend to be highly cognizant of their context such as people around them when they make decisions and, because of this, the Westerners' strong inclination to a type of rule-based categorization does not always apply to their Asian counterpart. Nisbett's work supports the argument that Korean's emphasis on relationship and community could help them adapt to similar cultural contexts of develop-

---

71. Chen and Starosta, *Foundations*, 50–51.
72. Nisbett, *Geography of Thought*, 61.
73. Ibid., 162.

ing countries in Africa, Asia, and Latin America, potentially minimizing culture shock and improving their work with locals. However, as in Hall's case, Nisbett's study has a danger of perpetuating cultural stereotypes and ignoring the complex nature of our globalizing cultures.

Second, in my international research, I have noticed that building emotional solidarity with people in developing countries is one of the most prevalent phenomena within the Korean humanitarian mission. This emotional solidarity seems to derive from Koreans' genuine sympathy based on their own experience of war, famine, conflict, democratization, and economic development. Most locals in mission fields therefore have less difficulty in accepting Korean missionaries when compared to Western missionaries, who may struggle with "their own postcolonial guilt as well as a perception of their being imperialistic."[74] Many Koreans, especially those who experienced the Korean War, believe that South Korea can be a good example for economic development. They thus often encourage people in the developing countries to learn from the Korean case. On the flip side, however, this type of emotional solidarity always takes the risk of being paternalistic in their humanitarian mission approach. For example, during my trips to five different countries in Africa (Cameroon, Ivory Coast, Burkina Faso, Ethiopia, and Uganda) with KFHI's Dr. Chung in 2008, I observed that he often included the following statement in his public speech:

> My dear African brothers and sisters, I come from a country called South Korea that experienced a devastating war and poverty only six decades ago. By the grace of God, many Koreans accepted Christian faith, studied hard, and worked tirelessly to get out of poverty. Look at South Korea now. Koreans have accomplished a marvelous economic growth. Korea has become one of the most developed countries in the world and it is now sending thousands of missionaries. If you accept Christ and live a transformed life like many Koreans did, God will bless you abundantly.

The above statement poses a potential danger of imposing Korean cultural, economic values on locals, instead of encouraging them to develop their own context-appropriate development model. Therefore, Korean missionaries need to be mindful that our contemporary mission context

74. Park, "Korean Protestant," 61.

calls for genuine and equal partnership that fosters networks of collaboration in global mission.[75]

Third, the exclusive, dualistic mindset—as in the concept of "us and others"—remains to be an ongoing problem among Korean humanitarian missionaries. In fact, many scholars in mission studies have observed ethnocentrism within Korean culture and a complex web of "cultural, economic, and educational superiority."[76] One noticeable factor for the Koreans' exclusive mindset has to do with the important role that the Korean language and culture play. For example, Korean expatriates around the world gather regularly to worship in the Korean language with which they feel comfortable and share Korean meals exclusively with each other in fellowship. While maintaining one's own culture and language deserves to be respected, Korean expatriates equally need to be wary of compromising their identity as missionaries, who need to share the love of God not "from a position of cultural and economic power, but from vulnerability and humility."[77] Here a well-respected practical theologian Emmanuel Lartey's work can shed light on the Korean case. Lartey, in his book *In Living Color: An Intercultural Approach to Pastoral Care and Counseling*, applies Kluchohn and Murray's formation of human personhood to the area of pastoral and practical theology: that is, every human person is (a) like all others, (b) like some others, and (c) like no others.[78] Lartey's demand for the well-rounded human understanding—universal, cultural, and unique dimensions—appears to be particularly relevant to many Korean NGO missionaries. In other words, Korean missionaries need to cultivate the multi-dimensional understanding of human personhood. In doing so, they can begin to understand both similarities and differences across various communities and individuals. To the same extent, it becomes important to remember that there are always Korean missionaries who are more accepting, tolerant, and open-minded than others for various reasons and this emerging diversity—depending on one's age, education level, intercultural exposure, personality, etc.—should not be overlooked. One step further, Lartey is interested in actualizing an intercultural paradigm in our multicultural world. Its ethos is grounded in an open, creative, and tolerant hermeneutics, which allows

---

75. Pocock et al., *Changing Face*, 249.
76. McNeill, "Lessons," 80; Kim and Khan, "Korean Movement," 123.
77. Park, "Korean Protestant," 61.
78. Lartey, *Living Color*, 34.

many voices to be spoken, listened to, and respected, while at the same time rejecting both extreme relativism and exclusive absolutism.[79] Lartey thus encourages us to take on any potential tension between contending positions in both active and creative manners acknowledging particularities of different communities and embracing respectful dialogue and engagement.[80] This call for creative tension and respectful engagement with others in dialogue certainly becomes one of the critical areas in which Korean missionaries need to develop in their NGO mission work across multiple cultures and faith traditions.

## What are the interfaith aspects of Korean Christian humanitarian NGOs?

In our rapidly globalizing world, it seems impossible to avoid encountering people from various backgrounds, and among them religion often becomes a critical area that demands attention. Many scholars of religion, especially since the 20th century, have attempted to construct ways in which Christians can engage in interfaith relations. The recent work of Race and Hedges, for example, aptly explicates various Christian approaches to other faiths. Here I will discuss four major approaches that stand out in conjunction with their framework: exclusivism, inclusivism, pluralism, and particularities. First, exclusivism refers to an interfaith approach that affirms the uniqueness of Christianity as the true religion. Jesus Christ is understood as the only conduit to salvation and other faiths are not able to experience God's saving grace through their religious practices.[81] Those who support this approach often see interfaith dialogue as an opportunity to convert others to Christianity. Many self-professing conservative Christians tend to uphold this approach. One major problem with this approach when it comes to interfaith relations is that it disregards other religious traditions. It does so with the strong conviction that Jesus Christ is the one and only savior, who calls Christians to convert non-Christians.

Second, inclusivism endorses the idea that God can be found in other religions as well because they are equally valuable, but only in and through Jesus Christ can people experience God's ultimate truth. This so-called fulfillment approach is based upon two theological grounds:

---

79. Lartey, *Pastoral Theology*, 124.
80. Ibid., 149.
81. Race and Hedges, *Christian Approaches*, 37.

Jesus Christ as the unique revelation of God and God's universal salvific will.[82] For example, many Protestant mainline denominations tend to promote this inclusivist approach. They emphasize the importance of having dialogue without ulterior motives such as proselytization, thus considering other religions as valuable partners in faith. However, they at the same time draw their limit in approaching other religions, which is to maintain the uniqueness of Jesus Christ. Karl Rahner exemplifies the inclusivist approach. Rahner, in his emphasis on the term "anonymous Christians," asserted the following:

> Those who are graced in and through their own religions . . . are already Christians and are directed toward what Christians have in Jesus. But they don't realize it yet. They are Christians without the name of Christians: anonymous Christians.[83]

Although the inclusivist approach sees potential in other religions and seeks respectful dialogue with them, it also has weaknesses in terms of interfaith relations. For example, because this approach still affirms Jesus Christ as the ultimate redeemer of the world, it does not necessarily lead to a two-way, reciprocal interfaith engagement.

Thirdly, pluralism is an approach that values mutual, dialogical, and intersubjective dynamics across different religious traditions.[84] Those who take this approach do not necessarily underscore the uniqueness and universality of Jesus Christ. Rather, they believe that all religions are equally meaningful and could lead us to the truth of God. One important theologian who represents the pluralistic approach is John Hick. Hick proposes a paradigm shift from "a Christianity-centered or Jesus-centered" to "a God-centered model."[85] Hick encourages believers of all faiths to help each other along their spiritual journey toward God. When it comes to interfaith relations, the pluralistic approach has the potential to genuinely respect other religious traditions and acknowledge them as mutual partners. However, its relativistic inclination could lead some people to question its Christian identity.

Finally, the "particularities" approach, coming out of a postmodern and postliberal worldview, embraces diversity of all religions. It supports the uniqueness of each faith and understands the Holy Spirit as a binding

---

82. Ibid., 63.
83. Knitter, *Introducing*, 68.
84. Race and Hedges, *Christian Approaches*, 85.
85. Knitter, *Introducing*, 113.

entity that fosters respect and dignity.[86] For example, Raimon Panikkar criticizes John Hick for suggesting "one neat common denominator" that unifies a variety of religious traditions.[87] Panikkar argues that instead of downplaying diversity embedded in each religion we need to emphasize the uniqueness of Jesus and the uniqueness of other religious figures. Paul Knitter, through his interfaith approach called "the acceptance model" clarifies that God loves diversity and, because of this, we need to accept and respect the otherness or differences of our neighbors including believers of all faiths.[88] Knitter asserts the significance of having a practical and globally responsible interfaith dialogue in which people of all faiths promote love, justice, and peace together. This approach clearly accepts different religious traditions as mutual partners and values interfaith engagement. However, some might question whether acknowledging many absolute truths could potentially compromise the unique meaning that the word truth is supposed to carry.

Although Korea is a multi-religious context, promoting interreligious relations has been challenging. The majority of Korean Christians consider themselves evangelicals whose exclusive soteriology tends to undermine or even demonize other religious traditions.[89] For example, Park Hyong-Nyong, who studied under Gresham Machen, publicly claimed that "Christianity's most appropriate relation to other religions is not compromise but conquest."[90] The markedly tough environment for interreligious engagement in Korea is differentiated from some other Asian contexts such as its Indian counterpart in which ecumenical theology of interreligious dialogue has been developed and religious pluralism is widely accepted. Sebastian Kim and Kirsteen Kim, renowned Asian scholars in World Christianity, examine some of the reasons for this uncooperative interreligious milieu in Korea.[91] For example, they explain that Koreans' absence of any colonial guilt about treating other religions, combined with the overarching Confucian cultural context (e.g., valuing

---

86. Race and Hedges, *Christian Approaches*, 112.
87. Knitter, *Introducing*, 126–28.
88. Ibid., 239–42.
89. Buswell and Lee, *Christianity*, 335.
90. Kim and Ryu, *History*, 247.
91. Kim and Kim, *Christianity*, 196.

of loyalty to a particular religious tradition), results in the distinctive contours for interreligious relations in Korea.[92]

Having described the challenging context for interreligious engagement in Korea, I further explore some of the ways in which Korean Christian humanitarian NGOs have dealt with the issue of interfaith relations.

First, the interfaith collaboration taking on global challenges has begun to emerge in the wake of the rise of faith-based humanitarian NGOs in Korea. For example, KFHI staff in Yaounde, Cameroon work closely with their local Muslim leaders to improve health and education. During my month-long research trip in West Africa in 2008 with KFHI executives including Dr. Chung, I had an opportunity to visit a small village with predominantly Muslim population located near Yaounde, Cameroon. This was the time when I got acquainted with KFHI's Ms. Suh Ji-Hye who had been working in Cameroon for ten years. Her ministry is supported by both KFHI and her home Presbyterian church in Busan, Korea. Suh has been involved in three different projects. First, she coordinates child development programs in partnership with local schools. Funded by KFHI, she provides them with school supplies and textbooks. Secondly, Suh assists a program called "Love without Regrets" that is designed to prevent HIV/AIDS among youth and to care for children and youth who are already affected by HIV/AIDS. In collaboration with local schools, she helps educate students about HIV/AIDS and attempts to meet the needs of the children by providing medicine and making visitations. Finally, Suh undertakes a program called "Missionary Medical Messenger" with the help of a group of Christian medical professionals in Korea. Through this program, she aims to train Cameroonian medical professionals who could potentially serve the community in Yaounde. Based on my observations, it was evident that she had earned a great amount of trust from locals who were mostly Muslim. For example, Suh introduced me to the local chief—a devout Muslim leader—of the village who resided in a huge, grandiose hut. Suh mentioned that she and the local Muslim chief had been working together to better the quality of education and health in the village. The charismatic local, Muslim chief wholeheartedly welcomed her and me (her guest). I was impressed to see how much trust she gained from the locals. Also, during my visit, I had a chance to meet with a Christian medical mission team from Korea, which was composed of twenty-five medical professionals. The Korean

---

92. Ibid.

medical mission team, a partner with KFHI, stayed there for about two weeks performing a variety of surgeries and giving out boxes of medical supplies to the community. Although I do not have a first-hand account as regards GN's interfaith collaboration, there is no doubt that GN wants to be defined as an inclusive development and aid NGO that cooperates with people of all religious backgrounds as its CEO Lee clarifies: "We don't exclude people based on race, ethnicity, gender, and religious background. We are open to working with people of all faiths."

Nevertheless, the level of interfaith engagement clearly varies depending on the mission statement and funding sources of each organization. KFHI and GN, in this sense, aptly demonstrate the differing extents of Koreans' interfaith collaboration. KFHI states that it is a mission NGO, which primarily works with Christian churches around the world. This evangelistic motive goes along with its clear intention of improving the quality of human life in developing countries. Thus, this holistic goal allows KFHI to justify its public, secular funding whether it is coming from the Korean government, business corporations, or people of other religious backgrounds. GN, on the other hand, downplays their Christian identity by making it clear that they are not an exclusively Christian mission organization but a bona-fide humanitarian NGO that is faith-inspired.

Second, Korean Christian humanitarian NGOs' interfaith collaboration, however, does not necessarily mean their willingness to accept partners of other faiths as spiritual equals. When it comes to KFHI, its interfaith approach appears to fall somewhere between exclusivism and inclusivism in terms of the above framework of Race and Hedges. KFHI's official mission statement, which acknowledges the unique role of Jesus Christ as the only way to salvation alongside the significance of inviting people to Christ, clearly reflects some of the major characteristics of exclusivism. Thus, KFHI's field operations often include some type of evangelistic mission. For example, KFHI encourages and financially supports evangelism programs that include revivals and mission trips. Most KFHI staff members believe that humanitarian mission without evangelism cannot be sustainable because the basis of sustainable development is rooted in accepting and embodying the Christian gospel. This evangelistic tendency is not so surprising considering KFHI's organizational goal is to be a mission NGO that undertakes holistic mission. One particular example comes from KFHI's evangelism projects in the northeastern region of Uganda that partners with pastoral leaders from two traditional

Ugandan tribes called Karamojong and Teso. KFHI staff members in Kumi and Soroti, in particular, provide summer intensive theological courses for Karamojong and Teso pastors with limited education. While I was in Uganda, I had two different opportunities to teach Bible courses to about fifty local church leaders who mostly came from a Protestant denomination called Christian Fellowship Ministries (CFM). Each CFM leader has an average of one hundred congregants and worships at a mud hut church with very limited material and financial resources. None of the church leaders have a college degree not to mention a graduate level of higher education in theology. Most of them have their day job (e.g., farmer, carpenter, ground worker) and lead their individual congregation in the evenings and weekends. After noticing the need of theological education for church leaders, KFHI missionaries initiated a Bible institute in 2000 under the title of Africa Leaders' Training Institute (ALTI) and they have invited local congregational pastors to join its three-day-long certificate program that is held every three months. In doing this, KFHI Korean missionaries cover the entire cost related to the program such as food, accommodation, transportation, registration fee, etc. Also, KFHI supports street evangelism and spiritual revival events that are primarily organized by the Karamojong and Teso leaders. However, KFHI's approach to other faiths is often similar to inclusivism. For example, some KFHI staff and missionaries focus more on witnessing the love of Christ to their neighbors in need than converting them to Christianity. It is exemplified in the work of Ms. Suh in Cameroon with her Muslim neighbors as I described above. In other words, in spite of her firm belief in the uniqueness and universality of Jesus Christ, Suh attempts to respect and embrace people of other faiths without proselytizing them.

By contrast, GN's interfaith approach seems to be close to inclusivism. GN's situation in terms of genuinely accepting people of other faiths has often been complex due to the fact that they sometimes have to work with evangelistic Korean immigrant churches in developing countries. For example, during my research in Tanzania (2010) and Rwanda (2012), I encountered several GN field staff who coordinate development programs. They are all devout Christians, attend a nearby church every week, and work closely with other Korean missionaries and local Christian leaders. Because of this, some critics have attacked GN demanding a clear answer concerning GN's connection to Korean Christian overseas missionaries. In response, GN made a public statement and clarified that, despite being faith-based, it absolutely forbids any type of evangelism.

GN further defends its position by explaining that there are certain circumstances in which they need to rely on some Korean Christian missionaries who are knowledgeable about the context of the region. Here are some of the excerpts from the public statement:

> We apologize for any misunderstanding caused by some critics who have accused GN of being a Christian mission organization. We want to make it clear that GN is a UN registered international aid and development NGO and we do not proselytize. GN certainly upholds its founding spirit, which is to love our neighbors inspired by the Christian faith. However, our ultimate goal is not to convert people but to feed, support, and advocate for people in need around the world.[93]

It thus becomes clear that GN's emphasis, in approaching other religious traditions, is somewhat inclusive in the sense that it attempts to embody the love of Christ without imposing a particular belief system on others. In sum, KFHI and GN's different approaches to people of other faiths show that interreligious humanitarian partnerships can be undertaken at various levels.

---

93. See Good Neighbors.

# 5

# The Rise of Korean Christian Humanitarian NGOs and its Implications in Sociology of Religion and International Development

THIS CHAPTER EXAMINES KFHI and GN, utilizing tools derived from social science, particularly sociology of religion and religion and development. It discusses the phenomenon of emerging Korean Christian humanitarian NGOs from various perspectives, which include four sections: the growth of Korean Christian humanitarian NGOs and its socio-religious implications, religion and its role in international aid and development, similarities and differences between Korean Christian humanitarian NGOs and their American counterparts, and comprehensive community development of Korean NGO missionaries through a case study of KFHI's mission in Uganda.

## THE GROWTH OF KOREAN CHRISTIAN HUMANITARIAN NGOS AND ITS SOCIO-RELIGIOUS IMPLICATIONS

What are some of the sociological and religious reasons why groups like KFHI and GN have gained momentum in contemporary Korean Christian mission? In exploring this question, I turn to two internal shifts in South Korea intertwined with the external shift caused by secularization, neoliberalism, and globalization.

## The Internal Shift and Holistic Synthesis

### Progressive values of modernity are mixed with conservative traditional Christian religious values: evangelism and social action as equal values

The first internal shift is couched in the ongoing tension between generally conservative traditional religious values and progressive, modern values. For the sake of argument, I narrow the scope of this first internal shift to one of the most contested areas concerning the history of Christian mission in general and Korean Christian mission in particular: evangelism and social action. Here I particularly consider evangelism as one of the most representative, traditional religious values concerning Christian mission, while at the same time considering social action as an emerging progressive value impacted by modernity. Having circumscribed the boundary of this internal shift, what is observed in the mission enterprises of KFHI seems to me an equal emphasis on both values. It is true that on the surface level the latter—social action—appears to dominate the practical domains of mission within KFHI. However, a close examination reveals that they still strongly acknowledge the role of evangelism as KFHI's mission statement indicates. As a result, KFHI can render its cause palatable to both a wide range of Christians and even non-believers whose interest simply rests upon contributing to its humanitarian cause. This particular direction towards a dialectical, synthetic response of KFHI seems to be differentiated from what has been generally taking place in its American counterpart. One of the most salient schisms that American Christianity has shown in the twentieth century might be related to the argument between social action and evangelism. As a result of that, many seminaries and churches have been divided, often ignoring or downgrading ideas of those who disagree with them. For example, it appears that the division within Christian academic institutions in the U.S. is reflective of the two contending missiological models.[1] Furthermore, Wuthnow, in *Boundless Faith: The Global Outreach of American Churches*, considers the tension between evangelism and social action as one of the most visible challenges within globalizing American Christianity. He suggests two solutions: defining evangelism as social action and treating the distinction between the two as a unique phenomenon only found in the United States that has to be transcended.[2] However,

---

1. See Schroeder and Bevans, *Constants*.
2. Wuthnow, *Boundless Faith*, 243.

Wuthnow considers this dichotomy to be a deep-seated problem with which American Christianity is likely to be confronted for a long time.

### Korean cultural traits are fused with Western concepts: emotion-ridden communalism alongside utilitarian individualism

The second internal shift has to do with cultural ramifications in the aftermath of the rise of postcolonialism and postmodernism. This change is also connected to the solid establishment of Korean Christianity vis-à-vis the attenuating Western counterparts by which its Christian faith was initially influenced. At its inception, Korean Christianity adopted many forms of Christian practice from its Western predecessors. However, over the course of its development, Korean Christians have garnered opportunities to review, reevaluate, and reformulate their practices of Christian faith. One prominent example was revivalism in Korea. The first Western missionaries in Korea intended to replicate the revivalist tradition in Korea.[3] Korean Christians undoubtedly responded to this call for revival as the massive revival in Pyongyang (1907) demonstrated, which produced a group of well-known church leaders in Korea such as Joo Ki-Chul and Kil Son-Ju. Surprisingly, the Korean church, since the 1960s, began to hold some of the largest international revivals (e.g., the World Evangelization Crusade in 1980 with seventeen million people attending) without the assistance of foreign missionaries. In the process, Korean Christians introduced their unique spiritual practices such as early dawn prayer gathering and mountain prayer to Christians across the world.

To discuss further this internal, cultural shift, I focus on two major cultural concepts: utilitarian individualism and emotional communalism. Utilitarian individualism has been a recurring theme in the modern discourse of sociology of religion in the West. For example, Max Weber, having highlighted the significant role of ascetic sects, posits it as one of the most pivotal historical foundations of modern individualism.[4] Weber emphasizes its utilitarian function through his historical evolutionary theory.[5] Alexis de Tocqueville, a French aristocrat who traveled in the United States (1831–1832), made critical observations on the American *modus vivendi*. De Tocqueville views independence or self-reliance as

3. Buswell and Lee, *Christianity*, 332.
4. Gerth and Mills, *Max Weber*, 321.
5. Weber, *Sociology*, 1.

one of the most outstanding characteristics of the American ethos.[6] His work is still regarded as one of the most accurate and useful accounts to aptly capture American individualism. Moreover, Robert Bellah explains the importance of utilitarian individualism in American Christianity in relation to the spirit of sects.[7]

Korean culture, however, emphasizes the importance of being relational in and through a community. In building relationships, Koreans are encouraged to develop *nunchi*, which is to catch others' emotions and feelings without necessarily having verbal conversations. This is the particular Korean cultural context from which a sense of emotion-ridden communalism originates. Therefore, while early Korean Christians had to struggle with those two somewhat contradicting values, modern Korean Christians attempt to devise a relevant, contextual rationale within which their faith can be best explained, further diversifying, hybridizing, and indigenizing the contours of Korean Christianity. Having affirmed this complex, cultural shift of Korea, I believe Korean Christian humanitarian NGOs properly demonstrate one of the most appealing ways in which the two cultural components—utilitarian individualism and emotion ridden communalism—are intricately interrelated with each other. For example, each Korean NGO missionary staff of KFHI appears to hold a strong, rational autonomy in his/her particular mission context—whether it is managing a University in Uganda; programs for children with disabilities in Uzbekistan; food programs in Ethiopia; and women's rights programs in Guatemala. However, my previous interviews and first-hand experiences at the above locations show that Korean missionaries have a strong sense of emotional solidarity with the community they serve. This emotional solidarity acts as a motivating factor that facilitates their active involvement in the community.

## The Holistic Synthesis

Holistic synthesis is a term that, I believe, best captures the predominant ethos within Korean Christianity in handling the aforementioned internal shifts, as exemplified in activities of KFHI. At the religious level, Korean Christianity tends to prefer a holistic option that brings forth a certain dialectic synthesis, in lieu of siding with one particular position. Similarly at the cultural level, Korean Christianity attempts to engender

6. De Tocqueville, *Democracy*, 786.
7. Bellah et al., 245.

diverse forms of cultural manifestation, equally emphasizing both Western and Korean traits embedded in its Christian faith and practices.

Investigating the term holistic synthesis demands some background information within which this concept can be aptly explained in relation to holistic worldviews of other global counterparts and postcolonial hybridity. Many missiologists and theologians have observed a type of holistic worldview prevalent in many non-Western countries.[8] As Bevan mentions, the synthetic, dialogical model aptly captures one of the ways in which the holistic worldview is applied.[9] For instance, Bevans notes that most of the theologians who practice the synthetic, dialogical model are from the non-Western, non-European world: Vitaliano Gorospe and Jose de Mesa from the Philippines; Kosuke Koyama the Japanese missionary to Thailand and the United States; and African scholar Charles Nyamiti.[10] In addition, the emerging role of holistic synthesis in Korean Christianity is deeply interconnected with postcolonial hybridity. The major discourse concerning postcolonial hybridity centers upon three important postcolonial scholars: Homi Bhabha, Edward Said, and Gayatri Spivak. Bhabha articulates the concept of hybridity as a mechanism that disrupts the exclusive binary logics of colonialism (e.g., the dominant and the subjugated).[11] Similar to Bhabha's argument on hybridity, both Said and Spivak positively view the role of hybridity in their postcolonial discourse.[12] Furthermore, postcolonial theologians tend to interpret a kind of ambivalent intensity that hybridity creates as a source for transformation emerging out of in-between space, thereby promoting boundary-crossing as opposed to boundary-protection. They challenge the monolithic categories of gender, class, and race, geared toward the new situation teemed with cross-cultural, multiple, and hybrid elements.[13] One exemplary theologian is the late Kosuke Koyama, who worked to build a bridge between East and West. That is to say, he was something of a hybrid, a product of both worlds. His hybrid nature is epitomized in his missionary theology that is the product of a dialectic involving

---

8. See Lartey, *Living*, and Bevans, *Models*.
9. Bevans, *Models*, 89.
10. Ibid., 95.
11. See Bhabha, *Location of Culture*.
12. See Said, *Culture*, and Spivak, *Other Worlds*.
13. Keller et al., *Postcolonial Theologies*, 115.

such ingredients as propositional/narrative theology, experience/rational reflection, and Western/Asian values.[14]

In his *Democracy's Dharma: Religious Renaissance and Political Development in Taiwan*, Richard Madsen illustrates progressive religious practices in Taiwan that underscore global responsibilities and human interdependence. Madsen's work is important in two ways: it perfectly captures the holistic synthesis that I attempt to extract from Korean Christian NGOs such as KFHI; and it demonstrates a variety of possibilities for holistic synthesis across religious and national lines. One particular example, Tzu Chi, the Buddhist Compassion Relief Association, exhibits strong similarities to KFHI in that it promotes a vision of human flourishing—social cooperation and harmony with the environment as exemplified in its relief and charity efforts—while naturally opening opportunities to teach Buddhism.[15] What uniquely distinguishes Tzu Chi from its western counterparts is its diminishing of individual autonomy. Rather, it relies upon radical interdependence borrowing the Confucian concept of human organization as a large extended family within which mutual responsibilities, not human contracts, are actualized in solidarity. It demonstrates one of many, isomorphic ways in which holistic synthesis—as in KFHI's mission practices—is embodied in Asian societies.

## *The External Shift and De-privatization*

### THE IMPACT OF SECULARIZATION AND GLOBALIZATION

Korean Christianity, with its rapid growth in size and influence, has not been able to escape the massive surge of secularization and globalization. But new challenges have been brought forth as the society begins to recognize secularism and globalization. For example, traditional, conventional religious values are now countered by secular ideologies that question the function, usefulness of religions, and globalization has set forth questions such as the role of religion in the sphere of world-polity.

When it comes to the definition of secularization, Casanova's work is prominent in that he expands the term from a single theory to three different propositions:[16] (1) *secularization as differentiation of the secular spheres from religious institutions and norms* with special attention to the four crucial carriers of modernity—the Protestant Reformation, the rise

14. Morse, *Kosuke*, 273.
15. Madsen, *Democracy's Dharma*, 17.
16. See Casanova, *Public Religions*.

of the modern state, the rise of modern capitalism, and the rise of modern science; (2) *secularization as decline of religious beliefs and practices*; and (3) *secularization as marginalization of religion to a privatized sphere.* By making these three analytical distinctions concerning secularization, Casanova highlights the complexity of modern historical reality.

In terms of secularization at a global scale, Norris and Inglehardt suggest an emerging, global challenge with which the world society needs to deal.[17] They mention that the publics of almost all advanced industrial societies have experienced a rapid secularization over the past fifty years. However, due to the contrasting demographic trends between rich and poor countries, the world has become more religiously conservative than ever before. Confronting the expanding gap between the sacred and the secular societies around the globe and its implications for world politics, they predict that the role of religion will increase and it has to find ways to mediate tension derived from cultural differences, which will remain to be one of the major challenges in our modern world. This thus leads to the emerging, crucial issue of globalization.

John Meyer, a renowned sociologist, explicates the multilayered dimensions of globalization with a particular focus on world society-polity. Meyer's world-society impacts nation-states through three processes: the construction of identity and purpose, systemic maintenance of actor identity, and legitimation of the actorhood of such subnational units as individuals and organized interests.[18] In this world society, Meyer posits three major actors (nation-states, organizations, individual actors) who constantly seek models of their actorhood. Meyer's five dimensions of globalization include the following:[19] increased political and military interdependence; increased economic interdependence; an expanded flow of individual persons among societies; expanded interdependence of expressive culture through global communication such as music; and expanded flow of instrumental culture around the world. Meyer particularly delves into the fifth element viewing it as a striking empirical feature of the modern system: within the instrumental culture, the aforementioned social actors legitimize their roles and identities; and as a consequence, it creates a massive isomorphism among structured, social units

---

17. See Norris and Inglehardt, *Sacred and Secular*.
18. Lechner and Boli, *Globalization*, 87.
19. Drori and Krucken, *World Society*, 156.

and a great deal of internal decoupling.[20] Although Meyer's world society thesis has been critiqued by some scholars due to his view on the stateless character of the international system, his take on the isomorphic nature of world polity-society is noteworthy in that it explains why similar characteristics are observed among entities from various contexts. Meyer's study resonates with some of the similarities among KFHI, GN, Tzu Chi, and American Christian NGOs. In this, the burgeoning growth of faith-based NGOs plays a key role in solving tensions occurring in the modern world interlocked with secularization and globalization.

NEO-LIBERALISM

As David Hundt notices, South Korea has attracted interest from policymakers and scholars alike by moving from being one of the poorest countries in the world (in the 1960s) to the ranks of the ten biggest economies.[21] Hundt also points out the particular situation of South Korea in which the state and big business corporations (e.g., Samsung, LG, Hyundai, Kia, etc.) are intimately tied in its modernization process.[22]

However, the economic crisis in 1997 in Korea, following the collapse of the Malaysian, Indonesian, and Thai economies, called for a complete financial and corporate restructuring of the Korean economy. A series of government-led reforms were carried out between 1997 and 2000 in order to "allow the full extension of market discipline to every aspect of economic life within Korea."[23] Interestingly, this type of neo-liberal reform had been attempted since the 1980s but failed due to the resistance of the general public in Korea. In the end, this economic overhaul propelled South Korea to become a bona-fide neo-liberal state, further reminding its citizens of the daily-globalizing world society and economy.

The aforementioned economic shift in Korea certainly has affected the nature and philosophy of many Korean organizations at least in two ways: dealing with the newly imposed reality such as "structural adjustment" has become a daily life in many sectors of the Korean economy; and they have begun to take seriously the increasingly interdependent nature of the world.

20. Ibid., 167.
21. Hundt, *Korea's*, introduction 1.
22. Ibid., 6.
23. Pirie, *Korean Developmental*, 105.

The transnational enterprises of KFHI, on the one hand, reflect this rapidly globalizing mindset in Korea. On the other hand, given the nature of aid and development agency, which requires donations from both private and public sectors, it might not be a coincidence that KFHI's president Dr. Chung is the former senior managing director of the Federation of Korean Industries and a close friend of the former Korean president Lee Myung-Bak. This, I believe, potentially allows KFHI to function efficiently in sync with what both the Korean government and corporate organizations pursue.

De-privatization

Globalization is closely interconnected with international NGOs (INGOs). As voluntary associations of individuals grouped together for specific purposes, INGOs cooperate with international governmental organizations (e.g., the United Nations) and states in a complex but decentralized form. Boli notes that world culture in the world polity can be best understood through INGOs, which denote the structure of world culture and rely upon five world-cultural principles: universalism, individualism, rational voluntaristic authority, progress, and world citizenship.[24] In this sense, the de-privatizing role of religion and religious organization becomes noticeable in response to the growing impact of globalization. KFHI and GN then exemplify some of the most effective ways in which the de-privatizing religious organizations respond to globalization through INGOs, subsequently counteracting the impact of secularization.

What is de-privatization? Casanova asserts that unlike what theories of modernity and secularization have predicted, contemporary religious traditions throughout the world refuse to confine themselves to any marginal or privatized role. Rather religion joins to be part of the public sphere of civil society and reinvigorates the modern public sphere while cherishing the sacred values of modernity such as human dignity and freedom.[25] This ethos of de-privatization—the sacred modern values geared toward the public good—is encapsulated in Bellah's work in his *The Good Society: The Public Church*. Bellah claims that religious bodies are part of the public, mainly because of their involvement in the

---

24. Lechner and Boli, *Globalization*, 258.
25. Casanova, *Public Religions*, 233.

common discussion about the public good, which runs in tandem with our ultimate responsibility to a transcendent God.[26]

In the case of American Christianity, four social factors have contributed to its growing global involvement in promoting the common good through INGOs: the shrinkage of distances between the U.S. and the other parts of the world; the cultural flattening of the world; the organizational muscle in international faith-based humanitarian and relief agencies; the grassroots energizing activity of congregations themselves.[27] Moreover, the diversifying ramifications in the aftermath of globalization are aptly observed in American Christianity as Wuthnow probes with two sets of cultural and economic categories: "global monoculture, glocalized diversity, beneficent markets, and immiserating dislocation."[28] Thus, this complex dynamics of world society indispensably call for global interdependence at multiple levels—e.g., between nations and the subunits of nations such as governments, organizations and churches. Wuthnow notices that American Christianity has been greatly influenced by globalization and further plays a major role in other countries, U.S. policies and programs abroad.[29] Wuthnow's analysis of American Christianity in this sense sheds light on what goes on within Korean Christianity with regard to globalization and the emerging need of global interdependence, combined with the de-privatizing religion represented by faith-based international NGOs. Specifically, Korean Christianity attempts to resolve the inescapable quandary of modernity by using holistic synthesis as its method, thereby becoming public, de-privatized, and international through its emerging international NGOs. In other words, the changing socio-cultural landscapes of Korea somehow have propelled Korean Christianity to reshape its form and identity.

## *Conclusion*

In the past many scholars of religion have narrowly defined and explained the nature of Korean Christianity without seriously investigating the intricate characteristics embedded in it.[30] It might be true that Ko-

26. Bellah et al., *Good Society*, 179.
27. Wuthnow, *Boundless Faith*, 136.
28. Ibid., 68.
29. Ibid., preface viii.
30. Jenkins, for example, often treats Korean Christianity as if it is a monolithic structure when he highlights its growth in size and increase in the number of missionaries.

rean Christianity reflects the growing religious groups in the Third World equipped with some traditional, conservative religious values as Norris and Inglehardt statistically analyze.[31] However, being ignorant of the complex, hybridized tapestry of Christian religion in the non-Western world can be misleading. Holistic synthesis is a concept within which modern Korean Christianity can be best understood in facing changes induced by modernism, globalization, secularization, and neoliberalism.

The major internal and external shifts that I delineate throughout this chapter hint at the multifaceted shape of Korean Christianity. The internal shift includes: the traditional, conservative religious values versus the massive influence of modernity; and the reclaiming of Korean cultural traits through indigenization of Korean Christianity versus the sustaining primacy of Western cultural influence initially transmitted by its missionaries. I believe that the internal shift can be better grasped when coupled with the external shift: i.e., the pervasive influence of globalization, secularization, and neoliberalism has to be addressed. In consequence, Korean Christianity has devised the following solutions that can legitimize its seemingly confounding transition. At an internal level, the concept of holistic synthesis becomes one of the most striking features that represent Korean Christianity—e.g., the equal emphasis on both evangelism and social action, the conflating reality between Western rational, utilitarian individualism and Asian emotional, communal values. At an external level, impacted by globalization and secularization of the modern world, Korean Christianity promotes its public role in a de-privatizing manner catering to both religious and secular needs geared toward the public good. The interrelatedness of the two quintessential answers—holistic synthesis and de-privatization—is inevitable as I demonstrate through Korean Christian humanitarian NGOs such as KFHI and GN. Perhaps, the two Korean NGOs only represent a small part of the whole. Nevertheless, the increasing tendency of securing its niche in a form of international aid and development NGO within Korean Christianity has to be taken into serious further consideration in conjunction with its counterparts from diverse religious, political, sociocultural, and national contexts.

---

31. Norris and Inglehardt. *Sacred*, 240.

## RELIGION AND ITS ROLE IN INTERNATIONAL AID AND DEVELOPMENT

This section examines some of the current discourses in religion and development including previous research, the historical background, and ongoing arguments about dialogue and engagement of religion and development. It answers the following questions: What is the historical background of international aid and development?, what is the role of religion in international aid and development?, what previous research has been undertaken in the area of religion and development?, and what are the ongoing arguments about dialogue and engagement of religion and development? This overview reveals that a significant relationship has been established between religion and development over the past few decades at both academic and practical levels. I further explore some of the implications for Korean Christian humanitarian NGOs. I do so by answering two important questions related to GN and KFHI: What has been the relationship between religion and international development for Koreans and what lessons can they learn from the general discourse in religion and development?

### *What is the historical background of international aid and development?*

Discussing the role of religion in international aid and development requires explanations of several related topics. Here I describe the meaning of the term development, a brief historical background of international aid and development, and the proliferation of international NGOs (INGOs). First, while the term development has been defined and used by a variety of individuals and groups, its underlying historical meaning has consistently related to the following shifts: from kinship to contract, from agriculture to industry, from personalized to rational rule, from subsistence to capital accumulation, from tradition to modernity, and from poverty to wealth.[32]

The modern notion of development traces its historical roots back to "the rise of industrial capitalism in the late eighteenth century," which opened opportunities for people to pursue material gains and to promote such ideas as advance and progress in a capitalistic sense.[33] Within the

---

32. Edelman and Haugerud, *Anthropology*, 2.
33. Larrain, *Theories*, 1.

industrializing, Western context, development was used as an ideological concept that established "order out of the social disorders in the midst of rapid urban migration" that often caused poverty and unemployment.[34]

The second phase concerning the term development began in the mid twentieth century following the two devastating World Wars that led to a huge wave of independence movement and decolonization around the world. In this postcolonial context, the term development had more urgent, practical implications compared to the first phase. On the one hand, it was connected to the humanitarian motive such as reducing global poverty. However, on the other hand, it was related to a critical reality in which the Western colonial powers needed to find new, relevant ways to remain politically influential and economically productive in their former colonies.[35] The second period of development produced many organizational structures whose goal was to promote global common causes through financial channels. One good example was the establishment of the Bretton Woods financial institutions, notably International Monetary Fund and World Bank. Those global financial institutions controlled global economy at a macro level including "a system of fixed currency exchange rates, regulations on capital movements across national boundaries, and the institutionalizing of national economic planning to promote growth."[36] President Harry Truman's inaugural address in 1949, which suggested utilizing American expertise in science and technology in order to "stimulate growth and raise living standards in underdeveloped areas or the Third World countries," reflects the Western ethos during the mid twentieth century regarding the concept of development.[37] That is, they were inclined to understand poverty reduction as an outcome of concerted partnership between developed and underdeveloped countries with assistances from newly established international financial institutions and aid agencies. They thus overlooked the other end of the spectrum, "self-regulating processes of economic growth or social change."[38] Some contemporary critics of development therefore consider these development agencies and institutions as an "anti-politics machine" that has ignored and simplified important political questions

---

34. Cowen and Shenton, *Doctrines*, 5.
35. Leys, *Rise*, 5.
36. Edelman and Haugerud, *Anthropology*, 6.
37. Dilley, *Contesting*, 215.
38. Cooper and Packard, *International Development*, 1.

while intervening in development programs in agriculture, education, and health.[39]

The third phase of development began in the 1970s with a specific goal in mind: redistributing wealth through global programs designed "to meet the basic needs of the poor."[40] This shift of interest from economic growth to global poverty sped up as the previously state-oriented development programs became increasingly privatized with market-oriented, neoliberal policies. In this process, the Bretton Woods financial institutions began to lose their dominant roles in development, and international NGOs started to mushroom often replacing positions that Western states had occupied.

The fourth phase that began in the 1980s can be epitomized as fiscal austerity under structural adjustment. It was the direct outcome of extreme neoliberal policies that often compromised the fundamental needs of the poor. Specifically, during the 1980s and 1990s the International Monetary Fund and the World Bank enforced a set of financial reforms called "structural adjustment" upon many developing nations. It included such policies as "reductions in state spending related to social services, reducing the state role in the economy, selling off state-owned enterprises, and labor market deregulation."[41]

The latest phase in terms of development began in the mid 1990s as debt problems of many developing nations continued to loom large. Furthermore, the austere measures of economic development strategy, which had been adopted by the majority of development agencies and financial institutions, came under heavy criticism. Even some of their own respected leaders, including a former World Bank vice-president, criticized "the impact of structural adjustment policies on the economies and living standards of the poorer countries."[42] As a response, the World Bank modified its structural adjustment and began to implement debt relief and social investment programs in order to better assist poor nations. In this process, international NGOs have become more important than ever before, connecting different agents in international development including states, business corporations, private donors while reaching out to grassroots communities.

---

39. See Ferguson, *Anti-Politics Machine*.
40. Edelman and Haugerud, *Anthropology*, 8.
41. Ibid., 7–8.
42. See Stiglitz, *Globalization and its Discounts*.

Many scholars and practitioners who engage in international development have paid a great deal of attention to the dramatic increase of INGOs since the mid to late twentieth century. For example, John Boli notices the rapid emergence of INGOs during the twentieth century, from fewer than four hundred to more than twenty-five thousand between 1910 and 2000, with such characteristics as "global, diverse, and complex."[43] Furthermore, the following definition of INGO by the UN Department of Public Information explains the crucial role that INGOs play:

> As a non for profit voluntary citizens' group, an INGO is organized on a local, national, or international level to address issues in support of the public good . . . INGOs perform a variety of services and humanitarian functions, bring citizens' concerns to governments, monitor policies and program implementation, and encourage political participation of civil society stakeholders at the community level.[44]

INGOs thus undertake a variety of activities to accomplish above mentioned objectives: (1) They raise awareness on specific public causes; (2) they host and sponsor a plethora of gatherings; (3) they directly engage in grassroots aid and development programs in partnership with the local community; and (4) they influence "other actors in the world society" including inter-governmental organizations and transnational corporations.[45] While the work of most well-known INGOs (e.g., World Vision, CARE, Save the Children, Oxfam) relates to aid and development issues, they only account for a small percentage of the overall INGO activities. Boli's study, for example, shows that only 6.3 percent of the INGO population promotes such humanitarian causes and the predominant portion of INGOs is related to science, medicine, information, technology, business, and sports.[46] Nevertheless, INGOs, as legitimate partners in advancing global, common causes, have undoubtedly influenced other entities in international aid and development including states, business corporations, and intergovernmental organizations. Above all, the role that INGOs play in the community level has proven to be pivotal and

---

43. Powell and Steinberg, *Nonprofit Sector*, 334.
44. Ibid., 335.
45. Ibid., 337.
46. Ibid., 338.

effective.⁴⁷ They work specifically with "the poor and vulnerable sections of the population" and promote community participation for long-term sustainability.⁴⁸

## What is the role of religion in international aid and development?

Religion and international aid/development has recently become an emerging field as many Western scholars and development practitioners begin to broaden discourses in both religion and globalization. In this section, I examine the ongoing discourses concerning religion and development, further exploring some of the implications for Korean Christian humanitarian NGOs.

While religion is sometimes accused of bringing conflicts, it also has contributed to advancing peace through its active involvement in development geared toward peace. For instance, faith-based organizations offered approximately fifty percent of health and education services in sub-Saharan Africa in 2000.⁴⁹ In other words, peace-oriented philanthropy, namely activities of voluntary giving and service to others beyond one's family, is embedded in most religious traditions.⁵⁰ It is also an unarguable fact that religious people are generous and concerned about serving the poor and marginalized in their individual society and around the world. Religious congregations and associated programs in the U.S., for example, accounted for sixty percent of all charitable giving in 2000 and the total amount of donations to the American religious charities in 2004 was more than eighty-eight billion dollars.⁵¹ Queen claims that religious organizations might be better than their secular counterparts in quality due to the fact that faith-based service providers tend to be more "personal, caring, and engaged with the life of the suffering individual" and view all people as children of God.⁵² Whether Queen's remark is valid or not, it is true that religion influences the enterprise of development in diverse manners: to name a few, many Christian churches' resistance against Apartheid in South Africa; the Iranian revolution of 1979; and

---

47. World Bank, *Working*, 15.
48. Clarke, *Mission and Development*, 3.
49. Deneulin and Bano, *Religion in Development*, 1.
50. Ilchman et al., *Philanthropy*, introduction 10.
51. Gardner, *Inspiring Progress*, 131.
52. Queen, *Serving*, 1.

Buddhist monks' protest against the Burmese dictatorship.[53] Moreover, recent study suggests that religious organizations could provide broader services than their secular counterparts in terms of promoting rural community development. It is especially so when local governments lack either "the will or the capacity" to assist and mobilize their citizens.[54]

### *What previous research has been undertaken in the area of religion and development?*

As clarified in the previous section, religious organizations and missionary agencies, with their strong concern for the poor, unarguably play a crucial role in advancing effective and sustainable community development.[55] However, their involvement in development has long been invisible or under-recognized in the discourse of development.[56] Clarke suspects that the lack of recognition has to do with at least two reasons: first, faith-based organizations might be considered more as part of the local communities they serve than as external entities; and second, faith-based development agencies, especially the ones directly supported by organized religious bodies, choose to "position themselves outside the secular development sector" in order to preserve their spiritual, religious identity.[57] One notable fact, however, is that the religious organizations' involvement in development has begun to gain recognition among both secular and religious academics and development practitioners.[58] This growing interest in religion and its role in development has particularly taken place over the past decade.

The following scholars are prominent in the area of religion and development. Briefly, Katherine Marshall (2007) gathers various narratives of faith-based organizations engaged in development-related work. Wendy Tyndale (2006) relates the work of the World Faiths Development Dialogue illustrating thirteen different faith and interfaith movements. Jeff Haynes surveys the constructive and destructive roles of religion in development processes by looking into four major world religions.[59] Ge-

---

53. Deneulin and Bano, *Religion in Development*, 1.
54. Clarke, *Mission and Development*, 168.
55. See Luzbetak, *Church and Culture*.
56. Clarke, *Mission and Development*, 4.
57. Renzao, *Measuring*, 2008.
58. Clarke, *Mission and Development*, 4.
59. See Haynes, *Religion and Development*.

rard Clarke and Michael Jennings (2008) explore five types of faith-based organizations in development: faith-based representative, charitable, socio-political, missionary, and radical organizations.[60] Finally, Deneulin and Bano argue that development theory has to rewrite its predominantly secular script concerning its treatment of religion, further promoting dialogue between different worldviews.[61]

## *What are the ongoing arguments about dialogue and engagement of religion and development?*

Traditionally Western donors and multilateral and international agencies have been inclined to treat religion by: (1) focusing on the common element; (2) pushing religion aside to the private sphere; and (3) avoiding areas of conflict when engagement occurs, thus potentially alienating faith-based organizations and downgrading the religious foundations of their development work.[62] However, in recent years, many scholars have begun to promote dialogue and continuous engagement between religion and development.[63] To them, differences should not be an obstacle that hinders us from rendering potentially fruitful dialogue and engagement. For example, Deneulin and Bano suggest that while there are serious differences between religious and secular organizations such as women's reproductive rights and the ethos behind educational programs, we should not overlook that "opposite, liberating forces" often exist within the same religious tradition (e.g., opposing positions concerning the ordination of homosexuals within the Episcopal Church).[64] Dialogue between secular and religious organizations should not take place simply for the sake of polite consensus. Rather it needs to open to other possibilities such as the deepening awareness of each other with mutual respect while accomplishing common goals.[65]

---

60. Clarke and Jennings, *Development*, 25.
61. Deneulin and Bano, *Religion in Development*, 6.
62. Ibid., 162.
63. See Deneulin and Bano, *Religion in Development*, and Marshall and Van Saanen, *Development*.
64. Deneulin and Bano, *Religion in Development*, 157.
65. Ibid., 165.

## International Development and Public Religion

### *What is the historical background of religion and development?*

Historically, the growing interest and organized activities among faith communities in social issues began with "the focus of Catholic social teaching on development" and "the ecumenical work by the World Council of Churches" in the years following World War II.[66] However, viewed as inflexible, conservative, and counter-development force, religion and faith-based organizations were neglected by Western official donors and secular organizations who were ambivalent about their role in development—e.g., their potential tampering with the legal separation of Church and state in liberal democracy.[67] Similarly, development studies, heavily influenced by secularization theory, have traditionally neglected the role of religion.[68] Then, beginning around the 1980s, two strains emerged: Washington Consensus ensured economic reforms including structural adjustment required by major international development institutions, which brought forth both support and critiques from faith communities; and following the Jubilee 2000 movement, faith-based organizations began to realize the gravity of global poverty and the need to collaborate with other faith communities as well as secular development institutions.[69] Finally, around the mid 1990s, the relationship between religion and development turned to a new direction, spurred by the Millennium Development Goals and Jose Casanova's study on the rise of public religions through de-privatization in the latter years of the twentieth century. Wendy Tyndale gives the following reasons for the sudden interest in religion and development:

> First, due to the political need to address the risk of terrorist movements gathering support among economically underprivileged Muslim communities; second, as the result of the realization that they need to work jointly with other organizations to achieve the reduction of poverty; and finally, as the result of the realization that to ignore the spiritual dimension of life is to ignore the main driving force of many of the materially poorest people in the world.[70]

---

66. Marshall and Van Saanen, *Development*, 3.
67. Clarke and Jennings, *Development*, 1–2.
68. Ibid., 17.
69. Marshall and Van Saanen, *Development*, 3.
70. Tyndale, *Visions*, 169–70.

On the academic level, research increasingly examines the significance of faith in development and the work of faith-based development NGOs.[71] Also, on the practical level, numerous forms of engagement between religion and development have taken place: the gathering of three organizations, the World Council of Churches, the International Monetary Fund, and the World Bank, which engaged in a dialogue process over a two-year period; the Tripartite Forum on Interfaith Cooperation for Peace in 2005, which gathered states, UN agencies, and faith-based organizations; the Micah Challenge, an alliance of Christian organizations, which held a conference at UN headquarters in 2004; and the 2006 global assembly in Kyoto of the World Conference of Religions for Peace, which mobilized six hundred religious leaders to take action in their communities in line with the MDGs goals.[72]

While the aforementioned events are positive indicators in terms of emerging relationship between religion and development, there are certainly caveats that need to be addressed. First, the difficulty of communication is inevitable given the distinct ways of perceiving reality as well as language (e.g., Christ-centered worldview of Christian NGO workers) embedded in both faith-based and secular organizations. Second, development theories and strategies can clash between the two. Finally, faith-based organizations have been suspected of being largely ineffectual in terms of their evaluation process,[73] and this will need to be refurbished in partnership with the secular counterparts.

## What are the implications for Korean Christians humanitarian NGOs?

The emerging Christian humanitarian NGOs from Korea such as KFHI and GN and their active participation in global aid and development lead to some critical questions in light of the above information mostly provided by Western donors. For example, how has been the relationship between religion and international aid /development for Koreans and what lessons can they learn from the general discourse in religion and development? When it comes to the first question, the Korean government has been in a very close relationship with religious organization—mostly Christian NGOs—in its challenging of global concerns. For

71. See Tyndale, "Faith and Economics," 9–18.
72. Ibid., 24.
73. Tyndale, *Visions*, 170–75.

example, Korea NGO Council for Overseas Cooperation's brochure lists about eighty international humanitarian NGOs, and almost 50 percent of them are faith-based (predominantly Christian) organizations.[74] This report includes KFHI's partnership with Korea International Cooperation Agency. Another example comes from GN's partnership with the Korean government. In order to promote the Millennium Development Goals, the Korean Department of International Affairs has assigned a variety of its MDG projects to GN, which led to GN's receiving of an MDG award in 2007. Thus, the increasing partnership between the secular government and faith-based organizations in Korea is similar to the aforementioned examples from other developed societies. In terms of the second question, there are many lessons to be learned for Koreans in light of the general discourse in religion and development. These lessons have to do with some of the criticisms that many religiously motivated humanitarian organizations have received. One major critique has been the difficulty of communication between the faith-based NGOs and their secular counterparts due to their different understandings of human development. For example, my research shows that the ultimate human development for almost every KFHI overseas staff I have interviewed during my fieldwork (e.g., in countries such as Uganda, Peru, Uzbekistan, and Mongolia) is based upon supernatural, divine dimensions. In other words, they strongly believe that a true sense of community development hinges on one's spiritual transformation that subsequently affects one's outward, material life. Another criticism is the issue of inefficacy in evaluation that relates to the lack of professionalism. This might apply to some Korean faith-based NGOs to varying degrees. GN, as a response to ongoing critiques from its secular donors, has recently taken the direction of being more professional. GN did so by declaring itself as a development NGO and hiring both office employees and field staff with strong international aid and development backgrounds. In the case of KFHI, both its employees in Seoul and overseas staff are inclined to see their work as a type of Christian mission than a pure profession. In sum, the Korean faith-based NGOs, in spite of their increasing collaboration with the secular sectors, have experienced some challenges similar to their Western counterparts.

---

74. Korea NGO Council for Overseas Cooperation, *Brochure*, 2011.

## SIMILARITIES AND DIFFERENCES BETWEEN KOREAN CHRISTIAN HUMANITARIAN NGOS AND THEIR AMERICAN COUNTERPARTS

How different or similar are Korean Christian humanitarian NGOs to their American counterparts in terms of their characteristics? On the one hand, in comparison to their American counterparts, Korean Christian humanitarian NGOs have revealed similarities including the diversity in their characteristics ranging from an evangelistic penchant to humanitarianism. While on the other hand, Korean Christian humanitarian NGOs have distinct features, which are fairly uncommon among American Christian humanitarian NGOs. For example, the Korean NGOs show a hybrid propensity influenced by both traditional Confucian and modern Western values. In order to demonstrate similarities and differences between Korean and American Christian humanitarian NGOs, I choose World Vision and Samaritan's Purse. I do so because of their wide recognition as Christian humanitarian NGOs among the American public, especially when a type of disaster strikes in and out of the United States. Both NGOs, for instance, played a key role in mobilizing recovery efforts during the Hurricane Katrina Relief in 2005 and relief and development operations in Haiti in the aftermath of the devastating earthquake in 2010. Also, my previous research trips to many developing countries in Asia, Africa, and Latin America have clearly shown the strong presence of World Vision and Samaritan's Purse, both of which have staff and volunteers in almost one hundred countries around the world with an annual budget of 2.7 billion and 385 million respectively in 2010.[75]

Established in 1950 by Rev. Bob Pierce, World Vision (WV) is one of the most well-known Christian humanitarian organizations in the world. Pierce's initial goal to serve the suffering children in Korea has now expanded to nearly one hundred countries worldwide. World Vision deliberately hires local staff—as opposed to foreign expatriates—who are familiar with the culture and language. Its mission is "to follow Jesus Christ in working with the poor and oppressed to promote human transformation, seek justice, and bear witness to the good news of the Kingdom of God."[76] World Vision hopes to reflect Christ in each

---

75. During my research trips to Uganda, Tanzania, Rwanda, Kenya, Cameroon, Mongolia, Cambodia, Uzbekistan, Peru, Mexico, Guatemala, I noticed that World Vision and Samaritan's Purse had a strong presence with their focus on community development.

76. World Vision, mission statement.

community in order "to heal and strengthen people's relationships with Him and with one another by partnering with churches and individuals to encourage spiritual transformation."[77] Thus, World Vision clearly reveals its Christian identity. However, World Vision is not exclusively Christian as it does not discriminate and serves everyone regardless of religion, race, ethnicity, or gender, demonstrating God's unconditional love for all people. World Vision, therefore, does not support any evangelism or church-building program. Rather, the overall programs of World Vision seem to be almost identical with its secular counterparts, which include nutrition, maternal health, HIV/AIDS, malaria, water and sanitation, food security, economic development, gender equality, child protection, education, and disaster response.

Samaritan's Purse (SP) was established in 1970 by Rev. Bob Pierce, who had also founded World Vision in 1950. Pierce's mission was to build a Christian organization that responds to emergency needs in crisis areas by mobilizing existing evangelical mission agencies and local churches. In 1973, Pierce met Franklin Graham, son of the famous evangelist Rev. Billy Graham. Franklin Graham, following his trips with Pierce to some of the underprivileged regions of the world in 1975, saw "the poverty of pagan religions and the utter despair of the people they enslave."[78] After Pierce's death in 1978, Franklin Graham became the President of Samaritan's Purse and he is currently leading its international relief and development operations. Samaritan's Purse explicitly attests that the ministry of SP is firmly based on its statement of faith, which accompanies specific verses from the Scripture: the Bible as the only infallible, authoritative, and inspired Word of God (2 Tim 3:15–17); Jesus Christ as the only way of salvation (John 14:6); and the ministry of evangelism is a responsibility of both the Church and each Christian (Matt 28:18–20).[79] The official website of Samaritan's Purse introduces its representative relief and development programs that include the following: emergency relief that meets urgent needs for victims of war, disaster, famine, and epidemics; community development programs that help families become self-supporting; and evangelism programs that offer spiritual assistance by proclaiming the gospel of Jesus Christ through local congregations.[80]

77. Ibid.
78. Samaritan's Purse.
79. Ibid.
80. Ibid.

To demonstrate the similar diversity of characters between Korean and American NGOs, this section, on the one hand, examines KFHI and Samaritan's Purse (SP), which show the evangelistic penchant. It, on the other hand, draws upon GN and World Vision (WV), which focus heavily on the humanitarian motive.

First, both Koreans and Americans uphold modern values such as efficiency and transparency. The aforementioned four organizations, for example, require regular progress reports from their program sites and make their annual financial statements available to the public. Secondly, they all rely on certain Scripture passages (e.g., Matt 28:18–20, Luke 4:18–19, James 2:17) and believe in a type of faith-related development that transforms the community. Thirdly, both American and Korean NGOs are engaged in similar types of development practice. For example, KFHI, GN, WV, and SP have all been interested in promoting programs in disaster relief, micro-enterprise, water and sanitation, disease prevention, and children's programs. Most importantly, the growing theological diversity in terms of organizational goals is one of the most remarkable common denominators between the two. These organizational goals range from an evangelistic penchant to humanitarianism (faith-inspired action). Then what are some of the outstanding theological parallels between Korean and American Christian NGOs? WV/GN and SP/KFHI show different ideologies in fleshing out their belief in holistic mission, with the latter being more ecclesial than the former.

*a) World Vision and Good Neighbors: Christian's faith-inspired humanitarian action is crucial and evangelism should not be part of it.* World Vision (WV) introduces itself as a Christian humanitarian organization that works with communities around the globe to help them reach their full potential by challenging poverty and injustice.[81] Despite its explicit Christian orientation, WV stresses that it respects other religions and enforces a strict policy against proselytization as its president Richard Stearns explains.[82] Good Neighbors (GN), similar to WV's, states that it is a humanitarian NGO inspired by the Christian faith that counteracts a variety of global problems. In other words, God's love for all people through the sending of Jesus Christ inspires GN staff to offer service for the needy. GN, however, strictly prohibits all types of proselytizing in its

---

81. World Vision.
82. Stearns, "World Vision," 1–2.

development context and this runs parallel with WV's public denouncing of proselytization.

*b) Samaritan's Purse and Korea Food for the Hungry International: holistic mission can be best accomplished by both humanitarian action and evangelism.* Samaritan's Purse (SP) introduces itself as "a nondenominational evangelical Christian organization providing spiritual and physical aid to hurting people around the world since 1970."[83] SP assists victims of war, poverty, and disasters with the hope to share the love of God through Jesus Christ. SP explains its evangelistic goal amid humanitarian mission:

> We serve the Church worldwide to promote the Gospel of the Lord Jesus Christ . . . we are an effective means of reaching hurting people in countries around the world with food, medicine, and other assistance in the Name of Jesus Christ. This, in turn, earns us a hearing for the Gospel . . . our ministry is all about Jesus—first, last, and always.[84]

Korea Food for the Hungry International (KFHI), in this sense, shows some parallels to its American counterpart. Similar to SP's approach, KFHI prefers to work with local churches communities in developing countries. KFHI does not have restrictions or strict guidelines in terms of evangelism. Rather, as in the above statement of SP, KFHI seeks opportunities to share the gospel with the hurting people around the world believing that a true spiritual transformation can bring forth sustainable material development.

## *What are the notable differences between Korean and American NGOs?*

As the number of evangelistic and humanitarian NGOs from the non-Western world increases, the dynamics within the Christian mission appear to become more and more differentiated and complex. One example can be found in the newly emerging relationship between Asian and American missionaries. Jonathan Bonk explains the complex problem of inequity within the missionary community in which affluent Western missionaries often need to work side by side with their relatively poor

---

83. Samaritan's Purse.
84. Ibid.

Asian missionary counterparts.[85] Bonk takes an example of Kosuke Koyama, who poignantly describes the economic gap within the missionary community in Thailand:

> The gap between us was immense in all areas of life. We tried not to compare ourselves with the first class [western missionaries], and we tried our best, but how could we avoid this comparison? We were living right among them day after day! . . . Our most irritating problem was our most esteemed Western missionaries![86]

While the issue of economic disparity between non-Western and Western expatriate missionaries in general—Korean and American missionaries in particular—is a critical matter to explore, cultural differences seem to be much more obvious and widely discussed, often resulting in misunderstanding and tension for both missionary groups. Here I examine some of the most significant cultural differences between American and Korean missionary groups with a particular focus on the aforementioned Korean and American humanitarian NGOs.

First, the Korean culture that values hierarchical structures seems to run counter to Americans' strong belief in equal standing. In both GN and KFHI, each CEO is regarded as an authoritative figure whose opinion is hard to challenge. This hierarchical mindset is different from the two American organizations, WV and SP. Although both Richard Stearns and Franklin Graham are highly influential in leading each organization, their role is similar to a coordinator or an ambassador that ensures the direction and quality of operations. In a similar vein, one's age strongly influences Korean's hierarchical mindset, which derives from the Confucian principle that requires the precedence of the old over the young. For example, in implementing so-called "country elder system," KFHI encourages the oldest person of the group to guide its programs for a particular region. This illustrates how important the age factor is for many Koreans.

Second, Korean NGOs tend to lay great emphasis on group cohesion and harmony whereas American NGOs are inclined to value individual autonomy. Steve Corbett and Brian Fikkert address the importance of understanding various cultural value systems such as the role of the individual and the group in shaping life: for example, the United States has an individualistic culture whereas nations in the Majority World are strongly

---

85. Bonk, *Missions and Money*, 63.
86. Asia Methodist Advisory Committee, *Missionary*, 136.

collectivists.[87] This resonates with the fact that Koreans culturally value some of the collectivist attributes such as harmony and group cohesion. But it does not mean that American NGOs completely disregard the importance of harmony and group cohesion. Rather, Americans tend to believe that maximizing individual's potential through one's distinctive project ultimately contributes to harmony in the group. Thus, it is common for an American NGO to praise a particular individual and one's humanitarian project. This contrasts to the tendency of Korean NGOs that would give credit to a group or a community rather than particular individuals.

Third, one interesting characteristic among Korean Christians and Christian inspired NGOs is their relatively adventurous approach compared to other Western counterparts. This relates to their somewhat aggressive mission approach for which many Korean missionaries have become known, venturing into "the hardest-to-evangelize corners of the world even at odds with the foreign policy of South Korean government."[88] Trusting in God's supernatural intervention in their mission work, many Korean Christians operate on "just do it, the Lord will provide the rest mentality."[89] Compare the Koreans missionaries' adventurous approach to what Jonathan Bonk describes in terms of Western missionary affluence:

> Without ample supplies of money, missionary efforts from the West would be severely curtailed ... Western strategies, beginning with the support of missionaries themselves, are money-intensive ... Western missionary strategies and their concomitant obligations constitute a powerful raison d'être for missionary affluence.[90]

In other words, the aforementioned Western mission strategies that tend to guarantee financial security of overseas missionaries do not necessarily reflect the ways in which their Korean counterpart operates. For example, some KFHI field staff members headed to their individual overseas project site even when their funds had not been fully raised. They explained to me that this could eventually become a great opportunity to experience God's miraculous provision in the midst of need. This yearning for

---

87. Corbett and Fikkert, *When Helping*, 164.
88. Onishi, "Koreans," 1.
89. Buswell and Lee, *Christianity*, 180.
90. Bonk, *Missions and Money*, 48.

a kind of spiritual adrenaline rush has become widespread among Korean NGO missionaries, and it generally contrasts to the ways in which American NGOs undertake their mission. In other words, American NGOs and their missionaries highly value methodical planning, strategic implementation, and financial accountability.

Finally, Korean NGOs tend to prefer holistic, multiple perspectives on humanitarian mission in comparison to American NGOs' individualized, project-oriented development practice. For many Koreans, building and reinforcing an organic relationship among various projects matters greatly for community development. For example, a child development program at a particular location requires its partnership with other development projects such as AIDS/HIV prevention, job training, water program, etc. Thus, measuring the success of a single, separate project would not be as important as the collective development of the community as a whole. This may be one of the reasons why many Korean NGO field workers prefer to be involved in more than one community development project differentiated from American NGOs' emphasis on a single project strictly defined by one's job description.

In the final analysis, the term hybridity aptly defines the emerging characteristics of Korean Christian humanitarian NGOs. On the one hand, many Korean NGOs model after their Western counterparts such as promoting modern values, implementing similar development practices, and maintaining the internal theological diversity. However, on the other hand, the Korean NGOs do not completely abandon their cultural values and practices. Rather, some of the major Korean cultural characteristics have been integrated into their development practice such as the importance of hierarchy, harmony, group cohesion, and holistic worldview.

## COMPREHENSIVE COMMUNITY DEVELOPMENT OF KOREAN NGO MISSIONARIES: A CASE STUDY OF KFHI'S MISSION IN KUMI, UGANDA

To further explore some of the characteristics of Korean Christian humanitarian NGOs, this section highlights a particular context of Korean Christian community development. I focus on KFHI's community development work in a rural town called Kumi, which is located in the northeastern part of Uganda. There are currently twenty Korean NGO missionaries in Kumi, Uganda. The growing number of Korean

Christians in Kumi is interesting given the fact that there are only few Westerners in the Kumi region. This is largely because many Western missionaries and NGO workers tend to prefer more urban settings such as Kampala, Mbale and Soroti or communities that are directly affected by the notorious Lord's Resistance Army (LRA)[91] in northern Uganda including Gulu and Lira. My research in Kumi demonstrates that the role of Korean Christian humanitarian NGOs, which are sponsored by Koreans, has become significant in undertaking rural community development. Furthermore, it shows that the Korean's missionary enterprise is very comprehensive, covering a wide range of areas such as health (water development, malaria prevention, AIDS ministry), education (primary and advanced), and evangelism (church planting and training pastors).

*Introduction*

At first glance, it seems odd that twenty Korean missionaries live in Kumi, Uganda. Kumi, a small town with the population of forty thousand and about two hundred miles from its capital Kampala, is mainly composed of people who speak both Ateso and English as their first languages. It becomes apparent that Kumi has been neglected by its own government when one travels across the country in which almost all major highways are well-paved except the ones that connect Kumi to its immediate neighboring cities such as Mbale and Soroti. Many locals say it is related to the history of Ateso rebel activities few decades ago and the current anti-Museveni (president of Uganda) sentiment. At any rate, Kumi happens to be one of the least developed, rural parts of Uganda, and it is noteworthy that even major Western international aid groups and Christian mission organizations have paid less attention to this underdeveloped region of Uganda. My previous field research with Korean missionaries in Kumi during the summer of 2008 and fall of 2011 reveals the important, increasing role of Korean Christian humanitarian NGOs, notably KFHI, when it comes to community development in Kumi. This section examines some of the important roles that KFHI plays in promoting rural community development in Kumi, Uganda. It further explores comprehensive missionary enterprises of Korean Christians in Kumi with a particular focus on health, education, and evangelism.

---

91. The Lord's Resistance Army is a militant, rebel group operating in northern Uganda. Led by Joseph Kony, the LRA has trained thousands of child soldiers since 1987, perpetrating a variety of crimes.

## An Overview of KFHI's Community Development in Uganda

KFHI manages the majority of community development project in Kumi. They undertake a variety of mission programs in collaboration with local community leaders. In the Kumi region, KFHI supports the following mission enterprises. First of all, KFHI established International Development Institute (IDI) in 1994, which partners with Korea International Cooperation Agency that comes out of South Korean government. Through IDI, KFHI promotes programs in child development, AIDS/HIV affected orphan care, disease prevention, emergency relief, and water development. Currently, five Korean expatriates are involved in the IDI mission, which partners with a few dozen of local staff and hundreds of volunteers. Secondly, KFHI supports Kumi University, which is the only fully accredited university in Ateso-speaking areas of Uganda. Opened in 2000 by a Korean missionary couple, Kumi University has about a thousand students from all over Uganda and Kenya. Twelve Korean missionaries work together with one hundred and twenty local staff. During my research, many locals in Kumi expressed their gratitude for KFHI's involvement with community development. It seemed evident that KFHI plays a major role in advancing community development in Kumi and demonstrates the growing influence of Korean Christian mission through humanitarian NGOs.

## Comprehensive Mission Enterprises of Korean Christians in Kumi, Uganda

Mission projects of Korean missionaries in Kumi are very comprehensive by nature. I highlight three major areas among their mission activities: health, education, and evangelism. I describe a brief overview, followed by a case study pertinent to each area.

### HEALTH: WATER DEVELOPMENT, MALARIA PREVENTION, AND AIDS/HIV MINISTRY

Overview: In Kumi, KFHI's IDI handle the majority of mission programs related to health including water, malaria, and AIDS/HIV. For example, IDI builds and repairs water wells and boreholes to provide clean water for the predominantly underprivileged people of Kumi. In addition, IDI distributes thousands of mosquito nets along with malaria treatment pills each year by mobilizing its Ugandan employees and local volunteers.

Finally, IDI supports the ministry of Korean missionary Chung Ha-Hee, who provides physical and spiritual care for hundreds of AIDS/HIV-affected orphans.

*John Kim's Faith-Inspired Community Development:* John Kim has devoted his life to global community development following his retirement. Kim, a Norte Dame grad and former engineer for Ford Motor Company, has tirelessly been involved in multiple development projects including water, construction, and energy programs. He has volunteered with many mission organizations such as KFHI and World Medical Relief. To bring clean water for the underprivileged in rural Uganda, he has drilled and repaired more than fifty boreholes in the Kumi and Soroti areas in which water has become a critical issue for survival. Also, by promoting an emerging eco-friendly brick making system called compressed earth brick, Kim trains Ugandans construct their buildings in a more efficient and sustainable manner. Finally, John noticed that rural Ugandans' daily work is limited by the times that the sun rises and sets. He hopes to distribute solar panel units to rural Ugandans who do not have access to electricity so that they can utilize their extra time for studying and income-generating activities. Kim is a devout Christian whose development mission work is truly motivated by his faith. He underscores that local church leaders in Uganda have lots of work to do in addition to their evangelism and pastoral ministry. At a conference for fifty-five local *Teso* pastors, Kim gave an hour-long lecture about the need for pastors to be actively involved in community development. To concretize this, Kim requested those Teso pastors to send their congregants to his class at Kumi University so that they can learn how to assemble and distribute solar panels.

### Education: Primary and Advanced

*Overview:* Another major area for community development in Kumi is education. To promote education, Korean missionaries have focused on primary and advanced education. For example, KFHI's Child Development Program provides food, school supplies, and textbooks for children. Joy Primary Boarding School, a nationally recognized institution managed by a Korean missionary Kim Sun-Ok, represents the importance of primary education in terms of community development. Furthermore, Kumi University has been the center of Kumi fostering future leaders of Uganda.

Lee Myung-Hyun's CDP Work: Lee Myung-Hyun has been a missionary for almost ten years, specializing in child development first in a small town in Mongolia and now in Kumi, Uganda. As director of Kumi IDI's child development program, she manages programs for children in the Kumi District (Nyero, Olilim, and Moru-Ikara) along with her thirteen local staff. Lee and her staff reach out to schools in the Kumi area, assess their individual needs, and provide materials in cooperation with KFHI, IDI, and local leaders. Lee also connects nearly two thousand children to sponsors in South Korea.

### Evangelism and Ministry Support: Church Planting and Training Pastors

Overview: Most Korean missionaries and volunteers in Kumi are devout Christians whose mission work is strongly motivated by faith. In this, ecclesiastical mission becomes one of the most salient areas of KFHI's community development mission. Korean missionaries partner with local churches including three major denominational groups in Kumi: Pentecostal and Assemblies of God (e.g., PAG Nyero), The Church of Uganda (e.g., St. Barnabas in Kumi), and Christ Foundation Ministries (e.g., Olupe, Ogooma, Otipe). To support ministries of local Ugandan churches, for example, several Korean and Ugandan leaders have teamed up and initiated a quarterly training camp for under-educated local pastors through its Africa Leaders Training Institute.

Rev. Kim Chul-Woong's Church Planting Strategy: Rev. Kim Chul-Woong, a retired campus chaplain from Seoul National University Church, currently assists local Teso pastors in their effort to build churches in addition to supporting their ministries with finance and prayer. He contributes partially to church building endeavors of local pastors. Kim intentionally provides funds that are required only for roof-construction, which comprise about twenty percent of the entire building project cost. His ultimate goal is to give the locals a strong sense of ownership and to cultivate self-support.

## Conclusion

Throughout this section, I demonstrate the growing trend of Korean Christian humanitarian NGOs and their important role in international rural community development, which is comprehensive by nature. I did so in the light of my previous work and research in Kumi, Uganda with a particular focus on KFHI's mission. In closing, I want to underline that there is an increasing need for further research that studies rural community development of other Korean Christian mission agencies and humanitarian organizations. Also, it will be interesting to compare Korean's rural community development mission to its Western counterparts for the sake of mutual enrichment, perhaps in relation to Wuthnow's work on American global mission activities.[92] Finally, examining feedback from the local partners and beneficiaries—such as the rural, Ugandan community of Kumi—will help us critically reflect on the ongoing mission endeavors of Korean Christians.

---

92. See Wuthnow, *Boundless Faith*.

# 6

# From "Development or Mission" to "Development as Mission"?

MANY CHRISTIANS UNDERSTAND THE term mission as a concept that was initially entrusted to Christ's disciples when he commissioned them to share the good news with people all around the world. Christians have practiced mission in various ways ranging from "religious conversion to Christian belief through preaching" to "serving the poor and the marginalized without being vocal in faith."[1] On the one hand, the dualistic understanding of mission, namely evangelism and social action, still remains prevalent among a lot of Christians around the world. Those who take this position define mission as either evangelism or social action. However, on the other hand, there are also many others who emphasize Christians' involvement in both evangelism (word) and social action (deed). Within the holistic mindset, they consider international development as a serious and legitimate part of Christian mission. Those who endorse the latter position understand mission as a concept that continually embodies Jesus' mission rooted in love. They therefore seek to promote development initiatives that include human rights, health, and education while acknowledging the important role evangelism plays in mission. For example, Vinay Samuel and Chris Sugden examine the emerging trend among progressive evangelicals that fully acknowledges Christians' faith-inspired engagement in relief and development mission.[2] They pay particular attention to the recent discourse on development and mission beginning in the late twentieth century. First, Latin American

1. Clarke, *Mission and Development*, 2.
2. See Samuel and Sugden, *Mission as Transformation*.

theologians, notably Rene Padilla, Samuel Escobar, and Orlando Costas, initiated the evangelicals' interest in social action-oriented, holistic mission through their participation in the Lausanne Covenant in 1974. By publicly expressing the significance of the whole gospel, which focuses on social, political, economic, cultural, and religious contexts, they not only challenged the aforementioned, polarized understanding of mission but also legitimized the key role that development plays in the broad scheme of mission. Later in 1983 at the Wheaton Conference hosted by the World Evangelical Fellowship, the socially-minded evangelicals included development as a pivotal instrument that can help people actualize transformation—the fullness of life in harmony with God. In claiming development as mission, the term "transformation" becomes a recurring keyword for many evangelicals as Vinay explains: "Transformation is to enable God's vision of society to be actualized in all relationships, social, economic, and spiritual, so that God's will may be reflected in human society and God's love be experienced by all communities, especially the poor."[3] This so-called transformation model is grounded in the theology of mission that values "the lordship of Jesus Christ over every aspect of life."[4] It addresses and challenges a spectrum of issues related to contexts of poverty, injustice, economic inequity, and political oppression. Bryant Myers, for example, asserts the importance of "seeking positive change in the whole of human life materially, socially, and spiritually" after claiming that poverty is fundamentally connected to broken relationships.[5] Myers' transformational development thus emphasizes restoring relationships at various levels:

> Transformation must be about restoring relationships, just and right relationships with God, with self, with community, with the other, and with the environment . . . transformational development that does not declare the good news of the possibility of both personal and corporate liberation and redirection toward God is a truncated gospel, unworthy of the biblical text.[6]

The ultimate goal of Christian witness according to Myers is to help all people (the poor, non-poor, and the development practitioner) find their "true identity" and "true vocation" in the midst of "just and peaceful

---

3. Samuel and Sugden, *Mission*, cover page.
4. Ibid., introduction xiii.
5. Myers, *Walking*, 3.
6. Ibid., 36.

relationships."[7] In achieving such holistic values, the transformation model puts forward two biblical concepts: first, incarnation motivates Christians to engage actively in the secular world in the light of Christ's humility and sacrificial love, and second, reconciliation focuses on restoring broken relationships between God and God's creatures and between people.

On June 20–23, 1996, thirty-five chief executives of Christian relief and development agencies from sixteen countries gathered in Oxford, England, in order to discuss the current global trends, issues for Christian relief and development NGOs, and future directions of Christian humanitarian mission. This consultation played a critical role in taking the concept of transformation into serious consideration. First, in discussing current global trends, they addressed the following issues: global economy, political machinery, global communication, and global health. More importantly, they paid special attention to an array of serious global consequences that include a widening economic gap between the rich and the poor, socio-political marginalization of the poor, and increases in disintegration of communities. Second, they discussed the emerging issues for Christian relief and development NGOs. One salient issue for many was the role of spirituality in the world of development. Most participants agreed upon the evangelical view that development is "obedience to the Lord Jesus Christ in stewardship of creation and love for neighbor empowered by the Holy Spirit," thus being differentiated from their secular counterparts whose focus tends to be on statistical improvement and accelerated change.[8] They also expressed the emerging need for cooperation with other religious groups that promote the common, public good such as advocacy actions. When it comes to the issue of church and development, nevertheless, they strongly acknowledged "the gospel as the most significant force for social transformation" and "the church as one of the most effective grassroots organizations in the world."[9] Finally, the group envisioned future directions related to Christian humanitarian mission. One common understanding was the need to cultivate local community assets for development in contrast to the top-down, need-based method. This signifies that the emerging Christian humanitarian NGOs should collect local knowledge and wis-

7. Ibid., 19.
8. Ibid., 395.
9. Ibid., 396–400.

dom with great respect, build relationships with communities to locate local assets, and facilitate an exchange of local knowledge among the disenfranchised. They further discussed the future of Christian NGOs, predicting that the consequences of the globalizing economy with strong capitalistic, privatizing inclinations could eventually leave many groups marginalized. In confronting this complex reality, the participants called for a Christo-centric perspective in which Christian humanitarian NGOs make intentional efforts to stand with and care for those who are "left by the side of the road."[10]

Interrelating the two terms, development and mission, certainly pose some challenges, especially due to some of the different historical backgrounds and assumptions attached to each. On the one hand, studies on development practices and theories began in the aftermath of the Second World War and have been primarily formulated by economists, "all strongly influenced by the ideas of Keynes and the post-war practices of state intervention in the economy."[11] On the other hand, the term mission has been mostly utilized by Christians and theologians, and it has often been used interchangeably with another term, evangelism, which is to propagate the gospel of Jesus Christ for the sake of spiritual conversion and personal transformation. Despite the differences, there is little doubt that development and mission have been closely related to each other. The growing relationship between Christian humanitarian organizations and their secular counterparts such as the government and business corporations has certainly contributed to this trend. As a result, it is getting difficult to distinguish Christian missionaries from international development and aid workers. For example, many Korean Christians who work for KFHI or GN are addressed as either Christian missionaries or international aid and development specialists depending on context. Because these two terms, missionary and development expert, are loosely defined, Korean Christians who work with KFHI and GN often use two different titles (Christian missionary or development worker) when introducing themselves to different audiences including church groups, government officials, and business representatives. It is equally notable, however, that those who work with KFHI are more likely to prefer the term "missionary" to "development worker" than those who work for GN who are more likely to be comfortable with the latter term.

---

10. Ibid., 409.

11. Edelman and Haugerud, *Anthropology*, 111.

## From "Development or Mission" to "Development as Mission"? 119

One example comes from my interview with Kim Yong-Sung, who is director of KFHI's International Development Institute in Uganda. Despite the fact that his work is entirely composed of aid and development operations, Kim mentioned the following:

> I prefer the term "missionary" to "development worker" ... not that I think the latter is wrong, but because I see my Christian faith as the center of my identity. Also it is the one that has motivated me to come here and serve Ugandans. To me, the former is related to a divine calling whereas the latter sounds more like a secular profession.

Kim's response is differentiated from the one that Kim Do-Kyung, a GN staff who oversees aid and development operations in Haiti, explained during my interview:

> GN does not use the term "missionary" in addressing its field staff. Instead, we prefer the term "development worker" because it better reflects the nature of our work as an aid and development organization.

The above differences certainly have to do with KFHI and GN's distinct motives for and statements of mission, that is, KFHI's ecclesial mission and GN's humanitarian mission. Furthermore, one recent study conducted by Kerry Enright and Vicky-Ann Ware affirm that there should not be "a neat dividing line" between mission and development.[12] After examining case studies of Uniting World (an Australian-based Christian mission agency) in the Pacific region, they observe the convoluted nature of Christian mission work in which both development and witness are tightly intertwined:

> Both theologically and practically, development is a form of mission and therefore dividing mission and development is artificial and confuses frames of reference. A theological understanding of mission clearly incorporates upholding rights especially of people most excluded and vulnerable, the core task of development. It also requires that Christians witness to what they have learned and believe.[13]

Can international aid and development be considered as Christian mission? Throughout the dissertation, I make consistent claims that

12. Clarke, *Mission and Development*, 167.
13. Ibid., 170.

there is a clear growth of international humanitarian enterprises within the Korean Christian mission. For example, in chapter three, I propose that the characteristics of mission for many Korean Christians have become diverse ranging from purely evangelistic mission (saving souls) to holistic-humanitarian mission by examining the historical development of Korean mission. That is, Korean Christians have begun to underscore the humanitarian aspect of global mission beginning in the early 1990s impacted by rapidly changing socio-political, economic, and cultural climates in and out of Korea. Also, the chapter four argues that Korean Christians have become interested in promoting the public, common good and in this process diverse public mission theologies emerge and impact their actual practices as illustrated in KFHI's ecclesial mission theology and GN's humanitarian mission theology. Finally, the chapter five examines the changing dynamics of Korean Christian mission in conversation with discourses in sociology of religion and international development. This ultimately leads to the conclusion that Korean Christians' undertaking of NGO missions represents one of the most emerging ways in which Korean Christianity finds its niche in encountering the rapidly changing world. In sum, the short version of my answer to the above question is as follows: the rise of Christian humanitarian NGO mission in Korea has widened the spectrum of Christian mission, further opening the possibility of redefining the relationship between development and mission: from "development or mission" to "development as mission." Traditionally for Korean Christians, the term mission used to be synonymous to evangelization, which is to propagate the gospel to unbelievers. To many, mission outside the domain of evangelization of the world seemed almost unthinkable. Since the 1990s, however, development has played a major role in terms of defining mission, further diversifying dynamics of Christian mission of Korea. Thus, many contemporary Christians in Korea are able to see Christian mission as something multiple in its form. I have particularly demonstrated this transitioning of the practice of Christian mission through KFHI and GN, two of the top three humanitarian NGOs in South Korea. To varying degrees, both organizations show in what ways international aid and development can be carried out in conjunction with Christian mission. That is, KFHI's explicit identification with Christian mission is different from GN's implicit Christian identity—distancing itself from the conventional way of Christian mission per se—in order to circumvent any negative connotations attached to it. Here I further delve into the increasing debate on whether development work can be considered mission—the interchangeability of the two—among many Korean Christians.

How would KFHI and GN understand the two terms "development" and "mission"? Some of the answers from my interviews with the CEOs of each organization below show two different understandings of which development becomes mission. What came up the most in my interviews with KFHI staff—both in Seoul and overseas—can be summed up as follows:

> We believe that development plays a major part in actualizing Christian mission. However, our ultimate goal is to accomplish holistic mission, which emphasizes on both physical and spiritual dimensions of human development. Development without sharing the gospel is not the direction that we desire as a mission organization.

KFHI thus wants to be identified as a Christian organization that works closely with global churches that challenge a variety of problems such as physical and spiritual hungers of the world. Within this mindset, development plays a major role in accomplishing its holistic mission. To the same extent, my previous interviews with GN's staff can also lead to the following summary statement:

> We understand that development becomes one of the most critical ways to undertake Christian mission. However, considering historically negative connotations related to the word mission, we refuse to be simplistically categorized as a Christian mission NGO. Rather we see ourselves as an aid and development NGO that is strongly inspired by Christian faith.

GN, therefore, tries not to be exclusively Christian in its development operations seeking supports from the secular sectors, thus considering development as mission, but not in the evangelistic, conventional sense of mission.

In sum, both KFHI and GN show that development has already become a crucial factor in understanding contemporary Korean mission practices. Therefore, separating development from mission seems to disregard the changing reality of Korean mission. Instead, the direction of Korean mission has become diverse, acknowledging development as mission in the process. The emerging model of development as mission nevertheless comes in many ways: ranging from KFHI's explicit mission that couples development with evangelism to GN's implicit mission that entails faith-inspired development operations. In conclusion, the emerging Korean NGO mission opens a new arena in which development itself can be identified with Christian mission to varying degrees depending on how Korean NGO groups interpret and implement the concept of development as mission in their practices.

Before closing this dissertation, I want to highlight one significant theme community empowerment,[14] which has become a popular development strategy in recent years among international financial institutions, multilateral agencies, national governments, and NGOs.[15] More importantly, Korean NGOs should study and implement community empowerment in order to improve their practice of development as mission, particularly considering the short history of international development from Korea and its lack of focus on host communities in developing countries. INGOs' implementation of community empowerment has proven to be effective in improving the lives of the poor for various reasons. First, focusing on community empowerment can help local, host communities take ownership and become active agents for development in contrast to passive beneficiaries.[16] Also, development programs centered upon community empowerment can be sustainable because they encourage local communities to be actively involved in all stages of community development including needs analysis, project identification, implementation, monitoring, and evaluation.[17]

According to Myers, Christian development workers need to be mindful of several important principles for community empowerment. First of all, they have to learn to respect local knowledge and let the local community become a genuine partner in the ministry. One of the most effective ways to put this principle into practice is to listen attentively with humility and an open heart.[18] Secondly, they need to replace their "traditional management-by-objectives approach"[19] with "a people-centered approach"[20] Only with the shift of mindset toward building genuine relationships with people can Christian development workers help culti-

---

14. Clarke, *Mission and Development*, 3.
15. See Stiglitz, "Role."
16. See Kirk, *What is Mission?*
17. See Dale, *Development*.
18. Koyama, *Waterbuffalo Theology*, 90.
19. See Myers, "Beyond."
20. Chambers, *Whose*, 147.

## From "Development or Mission" to "Development as Mission"?

vate community empowerment. Thirdly, Christian development workers have to remind themselves that the quality of local participation matters.[21] Norman Uphoff, a development expert at Cornell University, mentions that "the value of participation depends upon what kind it is (e.g., planning, implementing, and evaluating), under what circumstances it is taking place (e.g., central and genuine or occasional and formalistic) and by and for whom (e.g., local leaders, agency staff, and the poor)."[22] The ultimate objective of promoting local participation is to empower the local community so that they can build capacity and sustainability. Finally, Christian development workers have to learn to be good neighbors. They often get caught up in accomplishing specific development goals while overlooking the importance of building relationships with locals. This resonates with Koyama's so-called "neighborology" as Myers highlights:

> We must learn to speak our neighbor's language ... We must come to know what makes our neighbor laugh and cry. Once we come to love our neighbor, we realize that our love is rooted in the pain of God, the pain God feels when our neighbor is not loved.[23]

In other words, their mission is not simply about managing programs and teaching skills, but also about building relationships in the community.

There are at least two ways to put the concept of community empowerment into practice: *Asset-Based Community Development* and *Participatory Analysis for Community Action*. First, asset-based community development is internally focused in the sense that development begins from within the community. It is committed to locate a community's available capacities, skills, and assets, which include "individuals, associations, and institutions."[24] The asset-based community development seeks to maximize power and effectiveness for development by connecting the discovered local assets with one another.[25] Therefore, it challenges the prevailing, need-based community development, which focuses on community's needs, lack of resources, and problems. Those who support the asset-based approach criticize the need-based approach for its simplistic, problem-solving propensity, which could perpetuate the cycle of

---

21. Myers, *Walking*, 147.
22. Uphoff et al., *Feasibility*, 281.
23. Myers, *Walking*, 150.
24. Kretzmann and McKnight, *Building Communities*, 7.
25. Ibid., 5.

dependency and incapacitate sustainable change and community development. Secondly, participatory analysis for community action is another outstanding method that could actualize community empowerment in development. Originally devised by the Peace Corps for its American volunteers, it promotes four basic tools geared toward participatory community development: community mapping (resources, activity centers, institutions), seasonal calendars (labor activities, weather patterns, social events), daily activity schedules, and needs assessment.[26] Those who advocate this approach believe that its clear interest in the host community has potential to bring forth a sustainable and relationship-oriented community development. If Korean Christian humanitarian NGOs, such as KFHI and GN, hope to improve the quality of their humanitarian mission and ensure long-term sustainable development, they will need to study, practice, and build upon the aforementioned community development approaches for empowerment.

---

26. Peace Corps, "Community Mapping," 31.

# Bibliography

Armerding, Carl Edwin, and W. Ward Gasque. *Handbook of Biblical Prophecy*. Grand Rapids: Baker, 1978.
Asia Methodist Advisory Committee. *Missionary Service in Asia Today*. Kuala Lumpur: University of Malaysia, 1971.
Atherton, John. *Public Theology for Changing Times*. London: Society for Promoting Christian Knowledge, 2000.
Bass, C. B. *Backgrounds to Dispensationalism*. Grand Rapids: Eerdmans, 1960.
Bassham, Rodger. *Mission Theology 1948-1975: Years of Worldwide Creative Tension—Ecumenical, Evangelical and Roman Catholic*. Pasadena, CA: William Carey Library, 1980.
Bellah, Robert. *The Good Society*. New York: Vintage, 1992.
Bellah, Robert, et al. *Habits of the Heart: Individualism and Commitment in American Life*. Berkeley: University of California Press, 1985.
Berkouwer, G. C. *The Return of Christ*. Grand Rapids: Eerdmans, 1972.
Bevans, Stephen B. *Models of Contextual Theology*. Maryknoll: Orbis, 1992.
Bevans, Stephen B., and Roger P. Schroeder. *Constants in Context: A Theology of Mission for Today*. Maryknoll: Orbis, 2004.
Bhabha, Homi K. *The Location of Culture*. London: Routledge, 1994.
Boettner, Lorraine. *The Millennium*. Philadelphia: Presbyterian and Reformed, 1958.
Boff, Leonardo. *Ecclesiogenesis: The Base Communities Reinvent the Church*. Maryknoll: Orbis, 1986.
Bonk, Jonathan J. *Missions and Money*. Maryknoll: Orbis, 2006.
Bosch, David J. *Transforming Mission: Paradigm Shifts in Theology of Mission*. Maryknoll: Orbis, 1994.
―――. *Witness to the World: The Christian Mission in Theological Perspective*. Atlanta: John Knox, 1980.
Boyer, William, and Byong-Man Ahn. *Rural Development in South Korea: A Sociopolitical Analysis*. London: University of Delaware Press, 1991.
Browning, Don S. *A Fundamental Practical Theology: Descriptive and Strategic Proposals*. Minneapolis: Fortress, 1986.
Buswell Jr., Robert., and Timothy Lee, eds. *Christianity in Korea*. Honolulu: University of Hawaii Press, 2006.
Cardoza-Orlandi, Carlos. *Mission: An Essential Guide*. Nashville: Abingdon, 2002.
Casanova, Jose. *Public Religions in the Modern World*. Chicago: The University of Chicago Press, 1994.

Chambers, Robert. *Ideas for Development*. London: Earthscan, 2005.
———. *Whose Reality Counts?: Putting the First Last*. London: Intermediate Technology, 1997.
Chen, Guo-Ming, and William Starosta. *Foundations of Intercultural Communication*. Needham: Allyn and Bacon, 1998.
Chun Ho-Jin. "The Current Issues of Church and Mission in Korea." *Asia United Theological University Conference* October (1992) 1–5.
Chung, David. *Syncretism: The Religious Context of Christian Beginnings in Korea*. Albany: State University of New York Press, 2001.
Chung, Paul S. *Public Theology in an Age of World Chrisianity: God's Mission as Word Event*. New York: Palgrave Macmillan, 2010.
Clarke, Gerard, and Michael Jennings, eds. *Development, Civil Society, and Faith-Based Organizations: Bridging the Sacred and the Secular*. London: Palgrave Macmillan, 2008.
Clarke, Matthew, ed. *Mission and Development: God's Work or Good Works?* New York: Continuum, 2012.
Cooper, Frederick, and Randall Packard, eds. *International Development and the Social Sciences: Essays on the History and Politics of Knowledge*. Berkley: University of California Press, 1997.
Corbett, Steve, and Brian Fikkert. *When Helping Hurts: How to Alleviate Poverty without Hurting the Poor and Yourself*. Chicago: Moody, 2009.
Costas, Orlando E. *Liberating News: A Theology of Contextual Evangelization*. Grand Rapids: Eerdmans, 1989.
Cowen, M. P., and R. W. Shenton. *Doctrines of Development*. London: Routledge, 1996.
Dale, Reider. *Development Planning*. London: Zed, 2004.
Dayton, Donald W. *Discovering and Evangelical Heritage*. New York: Harper and Row, 1976.
De Tocqueville, Alexis. *Democracy in America*, volume two. New York: Alfred A. Knopf, 1956.
Deneulin, Severine, and Masooda Bano. *Religion in Development: Rewriting the Secular Script*. London: Zed, 2009.
Dilley, Roy. *Contesting Markets: Analyses of Ideology, Discourse and Practice*. Edinburgh: Edinburgh University Press, 1992.
Drori, Gili S., and Gerog Krucken, eds. *World Society: The Writings of John W. Meyer*. New York: Oxford University Press, 2009.
Dulles, Avery. *Models of the Church*. New York: Image, 1974.
Edelman, Marc, and Angelique Haugerud, eds. *The Anthropology of Development and Globalization: From Classical Political Economy to Contemporary Neoliberalism*. Malden: Blackwell, 2005.
Erickson, Millard J. *Contemporary Options in Eschatology*. Grand Rapids: Baker, 1977.
Ferguson, James. *The Anti-Politics Machine: Development, Depoliticization, and Bureaucratic Power in Lesotho*. Cambridge: Cambridge University Press, 1990.
Forrester, D. *Christian Justice and Public Policy*. Cambridge: Cambridge University Press, 1997.
Gallup Korea. *The Religions and Religious Consciousness of the Korean People*. Seoul: Gallup Korea, 2005.
Gardner, Gary T. *Inspiring Progress: Religions' Contributions to Sustainable Development*. New York: W. W. Norton, 2006.

Geertz, Clifford. *The Interpretation of Cultures.* New York: Basic, 1973.
Gerard Jennings, and Michael Jennings, eds. *Development, Civil Society and Faith-Based Organizations: Bridging the Sacred and the Secular.* New York: Palgrave Macmillan, 2008.
Gerth, H. H., and C. Wright Mills. *From Max Weber: Essays in Sociology.* Oxford University Press, 1958.
Gonzalez, Justo L. *Christian Thought Revisited: Three Types of Theology.* Maryknoll: Orbis, 1999.
Graham, Elaine, et al. *Theological Reflection: Methods*, London: SCM, 2005.
Grayson, James H. *Korea—A Religious History.* New York: Routledge Curzon, 2002.
Gutierrez, Gustavo. *A Theology of Liberation.* Maryknoll: Orbis, 1973.
Gwak, Chang-Dae, and Jurgens Hendriks. "An Interpretation of the Recent Membership Decline in the Korean Protestant Church." *Missionalia* 29.1 (2001) 55–68.
Hansen, Len, ed. *Christian in Public: Aims, Methodologies and Issues in Public Theology.* Stellenbosch: Sun, 2007.
Harnack, Adolf. *What is Christianity?* New York: Harper Torchbooks, 1957.
Haynes, Jeffrey. *Religion and Development: Conflict or Cooperation?* Basingstoke: Macmillan, 2007.
Hoedemaker, Libertus A. "The Legacy of J. C. Hoekendijk." *International Bulletin of Missionary Research* 19.4 (1995) 166–70.
Hong, Young-Gi. "Nominalism in Korean Protestantism." *Transformation* 16.4 (1999) 135–41.
———. "Revisiting Church Growth in Korean Protestantism." *International Review of Mission* 89.353 (2000) 190–202.
Hundt, David. *Korea's Developmental Alliance: State, Capital, and the Politics of Rapid Development.* London: Routledge, 2009.
Ife, Jim. "Principles of Community Development." In *Creating Community Alternatives: Vision, Analysis, and Practice.* South Melbourne: Longman, 1995.
Ilchman, Warren F., et al., eds. *Philanthropy in the World's Traditions.* Indianapolis: Indiana University Press, 1998.
Irvin, Dale T., and Akintude E. Akindade, eds. *The Agitated Mind of God.* Maryknoll: Orbis, 1996.
Jenkins, Philip. *The Next Christendom: The Coming of Global Christianity.* Oxford: Oxford University Press, 2002.
Johnson, Todd. M., and Kenneth R. Ross, eds. *Atlas of Global Christianity 1910–2010.* Edinburgh: Edinburgh University Press, 2009.
Jung, Joseph. "Renewing the Church for Mission: A Holistic Understanding of Renewal for Korean Protestant Churches." *Missiology* 37.2 (2009) 237–63.
Kang, Sungsam. "Basic Missionary Training: Bible and Disciple." *Korean Mission Quarterly* 8.29 (2009) 29–40.
Kang, Wi Jo. *Christ and Caesar in Modern Korea: A History of Christianity and Politics.* Albany: Suny University New York Press, 1997.
Keller, Catherine, et al., eds. *Postcolonial Theologies: Divinity and Empire.* St. Louis: Chalice, 2004.
Keller, Rosemary Skinner, ed. *Spirituality & Social Responsibility.* Nashville: Abingdon, 1993.
Kendall, Laurel. *Shamans, Nostalgias, and the IMF: South Korean Popular Religion in Motion.* Honolulu: University of Hawaii Press, 2009.

Kim, Andrew E. *Korean Religious Culture and Its Affinity to Christianity.* Seoul: Korea University Press, 2000.
Kim, Chang Tae, and Tong-Shik Ryu, eds. *A History of Korean Religious Thought.* Seoul: Yonsei University, 1986.
Kim, Germans, and V. S. Khan. "The Korean Movement in Kazakhstan: Ten Years Later." *Korean and Korean American Studies Bulletin* 12 (2001) 45–89.
Kim, Hogarth Hyun-Key. *Korean Shamanism and Cultural Nationalism.* Seoul: Jimoondang, 1999.
Kim, S. Hun, and Wonsuk Ma, eds. *Korean Diaspora and Christian Mission.* Eugene, OR: Wipf & Stock, 2011.
Kim, Sebastian, and Kirsteen Kim. *Christianity as a World Religion.* London: Continuum, 2008.
Kirk, Andrew. *What is Mission?: Theological Explorations.* London: Fortress, 2000.
Knitter, Paul. *Introducing Theologies of Religions.* Maryknoll: Orbis, 2002.
Korea NGO Council for Overseas Cooperation (KCOC). *Annual Brochure,* 2011.
Korea World Missions Association Annual (KWMA). *Annual Publication,* 2010.
Koyama, Kosuke. *Waterbuffalo Theology.* London: SCM, 1974.
Kretzmann, John P., and John L. McKnight. *Building Communities from the Inside Out: A Path Toward Finding and Mobilizing a Community's Assets.* Chicago: ACTA 1993.
LaCugna, Catherine Mowry. *God for Us: The Trinity and Christian Life.* San Francisco: Harper Collins, 1991.
Larrain, Jorge. *Theories of Development: Capitalism, Colonialism, and Dependency.* London: Polity, 1989.
Lartey, Emmanuel. *In Living Color: An Intercultural Approach to Pastoral Care and Counseling.* London: Jessica Kingsley, 2003.
———. *Pastoral Theology in an Intercultural World.* Cleveland: Pilgrim, 2006.
Lechner, Frank J., and John Boli. *The Globalization Reader.* Malden: Blackwell, 2004.
Lee, Moonjang. "Experience of Religious Plurality in Korea: its Theological Implications." *International Review of Mission* 88.351 (1999) 399–413.
Lee, Timothy S. "A Political Factor in the Rise of Protestantism in Korea: Protestantism and the 1919 March Movement." *Church History* 69.1 (2000) 116–42.
Leys, Colin. *The Rise and Fall of Development Theory.* Oxford: James Currey, 1996.
Livermore, David A. *Serving with Eyes Wide Open: Doing Short-Term Missions with Cultural Intelligence.* Grand Rapids: Baker, 2006.
Luzbetak, Louis. *The Church and Culture.* Maryknoll: Orbis, 1988.
Madsen, Richard. *Democracy's Dharma: Religious Renaissance and Political Development in Taiwan.* Berkeley: University of California Press, 2007.
Marsden, George M. *Fundamentalism and American Culture.* New York: Oxford University Press, 1980.
Marshall, Katherine, and Marisa Van Saanen. *Development and Faith: Where Mind, Heart, and Soul Work Together.* Washington D.C. The World Bank, 2007.
Marty, Martin. *The Public Church.* New York: Crossroad, 1981.
McGavran, Donald A. *The Bridges of God: A Study in the Strategy of Missions.* New York: Friendship, 1955.
———. "My Pilgrimage in Mission." *International Bulletin of Missionary Research* 10.2 (1986) 53–58.
———. "Will Uppsala Betray the Two Billion?." *Church Growth Bulletin* 4.5 (1968) 292–97.

McGrath, Alister E. *Christian Theology: An Introduction.* Oxford: Blackwell, 1994.
McNeill, John. "Lessons from Korean Mission in the Former Soviet Region" *International Bulletin of Missionary Research* 36.2 (2012) 78–82.
Moffett, Samuel H. *The Christians of Korea.* New York: Friendship, 1962.
———. *A History of Christianity in Asia: Volume II* 1500–1900. Maryknoll: Orbis, 2005.
Moon, Steve Sang-Cheol. "Missions from Korea 2012: Slowdown and Maturation." *International Bulletin of Missionary Research* 36.2 (2012) 84–85.
Moreau, A. Scott. *Evangelical Dictionary of World Missions.* Grand Rapids: Baker, 2000.
Morse, Merrill. *Kosuke Koyama: A Model for Intercultural Theology.* Frankfurt: Peter Lang, 1991.
Myers, Bryant L. "Beyond Management by Objectives." *MARC Newsletter* 92.2 (1992).
———. *Walking with the Poor: Principles and Practices of Transformational Development.* Maryknoll: Orbis, 1999.
———. *Working with the Poor: New Insights and Learnings from Development Practitioners.* Monrovia: World Vision, 1999.
Nahm, Andrew C., ed. *Korea Under Japanese Colonial Rule: Studies of the Policy and Techniques of Japanese Colonialism.* Kalamazoo, MI: Western Michigan University Center for Korean Studies, 1973.
Neill, Stephen. *A History of Christian Missions.* New York: Penguin, 1964.
Newbigin, Lesslie. *The Gospel in a Pluralist Society.* Grand Rapids: Eerdmans: WCC, 1989.
Nganda, Ssemujju Ibrahim. "Corruption Endemic in Uganda." *Weekly Observer.* Online: http://www.theguardian.com/katine/2009/mar/13/corruption-endemic-in-uganda.
Nisbett, Richard E. *The Geography of Thought: How Asians and Westerners Think Differently . . . and Why.* New York: Free, 2003.
Norris, Pippa, and Ronald Inglehardt. *Sacred and Secular: Religion and Politics Worldwide.* Cambridge: Cambridge University Press, 2004.
Onishi, Norimitsu. "Koreans Quietly Evangelizing Among Muslims in Mideast." *New York Times,* November 1, 2004, A1.
Ott, Craig, et al. *Encountering Theology of Mission: Biblical Foundations, Historical Developments, and Contemporary Issues.* Grand Rapids: Baker Academic, 2010.
Paik, George L. *The History of Protestant Mission in Korea* 1832–1910. Seoul: Yonsei University Press, 1987.
Park, Joon-Sik. "Korean Protestant Christianity: A Missiological Reflection," In *International Bulletin of Missionary Research* 36.2 (2012) 59–64.
Peace Corps Handbook. "Community Mapping and Seasonal Calendars." In *PACA: Using Participatory Analysis for Community Action.* Information and Exchange, No. M00086.
Pirie, Iain. *The Korean Developmental State: From a Dirigisme to Neo-liberalism.* London: Routledge, 2008.
Pocock, Michael, et al. *The Changing Face of World Missions: Engaging Contemporary Issues and Trends.* Grand Rapids: Baker Academic, 2005.
Powell, Walter W., and Richard Steinberg, eds. *The Nonprofit Sector: A Research Handbook.* New Haven, CT: Yale University Press, 2006.
Queen II, Edward L, ed. *Serving Those in Need: A Handbook for Managing Faith-Based Human Services Organizations.* San Francisco: Jossey-Bass, 2000.

Quistorp, Heinrich. *Calvin's Doctrine of the Last Things*. London: Lutterworth, 1955.
Race, Alan, and Paul M. Hedges. *Christian Approaches to Other Faiths*. London: SCM, 2008.
Renzao A, ed. *Measuring Development Effectiveness*. New York: Nova, 2008.
Robert, Dana L. *Christian Mission: How Christianity Became a World Religion*. Malden: Wiley-Blackwell, 2009.
Roberts, Richard H., ed. *Religion and the Transformation of Capitalism: Comparative Approaches*. London: Routledge, 1995.
Said, Edward W. *Culture and Imperialism*. New York: Vintage, 1994.
Samuel, Vinay, and Chris Sugden, eds. *Mission as Transformation: A Theology of the Whole Gospel*. Eugene, OR: Wipf & Stock, 2009.
Sanneh, Lamin. *Translating the Message: The Missionary Impact on Culture*. Maryknoll: Orbis, 1989.
———. *Whose Religion Is Christianity?: The Gospel Beyond the West*. Grand Rapids: Eerdmans, 2003.
Scherer, James A. *Gospel, Church, and Kingdom: Comparative Studies in World Mission Theology*. Minneapolis: Augsburg, 1987.
Scherer, James A., and Stephen Bevans. *New Directions in Mission and Evangelization I: Basic Statements 1974–1991*. Maryknoll: Orbis, 1992.
Simpson, Gary M. "Civil Society and Congregations as Public Moral Companions." *Word & World* 15 (1995) 420–27.
———. "God, Civil Society, and Congregations as Public Moral Companions." In *Testing the Spirit: How Theology Informs the Study of Congregations*, edited by Patrick Keifert, 67–88. Grand Rapids: Eerdmans, 2009.
Smit, Jan Olav. *Pope Pius XII*. London: Burns Oates & Washburne, 1951.
Smith, Timothy L. *Revivalism and Social Reform*. New York: Harper Torchbooks, 1957.
Snyder, Howard A. *Global Good News: Mission in a Postmodern Age*. Nashville: Abingdon, 2001.
Solle, Dorothee. *Thinking about God: An Introduction to Theology*. London: SCM, 1990.
Son, Myong-Gul. *Korean Churches in Search for Self-Identity, 1930–1970*. PhD diss., Southern Methodist University, 1974.
Soros, George. *On Globalization*. New York: Public Affairs-Perseus, 2002.
Spivak, Gayatri Chakravorty. *In Other Worlds: Essays in Cultural Politics*. New York: Methuen, 1987.
Stackhouse, Max L. *Public Theology and Political Economy: Christian Stewardship in Modern Society*. Grand Rapids: Eerdmans, 1987.
Stearns, Richard. "World Vision CEO Richard Stearns Charts Course, Spirit For Nonprofit Sector." *Huffington Post*, March 3, 2011, 1–2.
Stiglitz, Joseph E. *Globalization and its Discounts*. New York: W.W. Norton, 2002.
———. "The Role of Participation in Development." *Development Outreach*. Washington D.C.: World Bank, 1999.
Storti, Craig. *Figuring Foreigners Out: A Practical Guide*. Boston: Intercultural, 1999.
Suh, David Kwang-Sun. "American Missionaries and a Hundred Years of Korean Protestantism." *International Review of Mission* 74.293 (1985) 5–18.
Swinton, John, and Harriet Mowat. *Practical Theology and Qualitative Research*. London: SCM, 2006.
Teilhard de Chardin, Pierre. *The Phenomenon of Man*. New York: Harper & Row, 1965.

Tennent, Timothy G. *Encountering Theology of Mission: Biblical Foundations, Historical Developments, and Contemporary Issues*. Grand Rapids: Baker Academic, 2010.

———. *Invitation to World Missions: A Trinitarian Missiology for the Twenty-first Century*. Grand Rapids: Kregel, 2010.

Thiemann, Ronald F. *Constructing a Public Theology: The Church in a Pluralistic Culture*. Louisville: Westminster John Knox, 1991.

Tillich, Paul. *Systematic Theology*, volume 2. Chicago: University of Chicago Press, 1967.

Tracy, David. *Blessed Rage for Order: The New Pluralism in Theology*. Chicago: University of Chicago Press, 1996.

———. *The Analogical Imagination: Christian Theology and the Culture of Pluralism*. New York: Crossroad, 1981.

Tracy, David, and John B. Cobb Jr. *Talking About God*. New York: Seabury, 1983.

Troeltsch, Ernst. *The Social Teaching of the Christian Churches:* Vol. 1–2. Louisville: Westminster John Knox, 1931.

Tucker, Robert C, ed. *The Marx-Engels Reader*. New York: W. W. Norton, 1978.

Tyndale, Wendy. "Faith and Economics in Development: A Bridge Across the Chasm?," *Development in Practice* 10.1 (2000) 9–18.

———. *Visions of Development: Faith-Based Initiatives*. Basingstoke: Ashgate, 2006.

Uphoff, Norman, et al. *Feasibility and Application of Rural Development Participation: A State of the Art Paper*. Ithaca, New York: Cornell University, Rural Development Committee, Center for International Studies, 1979.

———. *Reasons for Success: Learning from Instructive Experiences in Rural Development*. West Hartford: Kumarian, 1998.

Valentine, Benjamin. *Mapping Public Theology: Beyond Culture, Identity, and Difference*. London: Trinity Press International, 2002.

Walls, Andrew F. *The Cross-Cultural Process in Christian History: Studies in the Transmission and Appropriation of Faith*. Maryknoll: Orbis, 2002.

———. "The Mission of the Church Today in the Light of Global History." *Word and World* 20.1 (2000) 17–21.

———. *The Missionary Movement in Christian History: Studies in the Transmission of Faith*. Maryknoll: Orbis, 1996.

———. "Old Athens and New Jerusalem: Some Signposts for Christian Scholarship in the Early History of Mission Studies." *International Bulletin of Missionary Research* 21.4 (1997) 146–54.

Walls, Andrew Walls, and Cathy Ross, eds. *Mission in the 21st Century: Exploring the Five Marks of Global Mission*. Maryknoll: Orbis, 2008.

Weber, Max. *The Sociology of Religion*. Boston: Beacon, 1922.

Weber, Timothy P. *Living in the Shadow of the Second Coming: American Premillennialism, 1875–1925*. Oxford: Oxford University Press, 1979.

Winter, Ralph D., and Steven C. Hawthorne, eds. *Perspectives on the World Christian Movement: A Reader*. Pasadena, CA: William Carey Library, 2009.

World Bank. *Working with NGOs*. Washington, DC: World Bank, 1995.

Wuthnow, Robert. *Boundless Faith: The Global Outreach of American Churches*. Berkeley: University of California Press, 2009.

———. *The Restructuring of American Religion*. Princeton, NJ: Princeton University Press, 1988.

Yamamori, Tetsunao, ed. *Serving the Poor in Africa*. Monrovia, CA: MARC, 1996.

Yates, Timothy. *Christian Mission in the Twentieth Century*. Cambridge: Cambridge University Press, 1994.

www.ingramcontent.com/pod-product-compliance
Lightning Source LLC
Chambersburg PA
CBHW072156160426
43197CB00012B/2404